# LAVENDER

# LAVENDER

### PRACTICAL INSPIRATIONS FOR NATURAL GIFTS, COUNTRY
### CRAFTS AND DECORATIVE DISPLAYS

## TESSA EVELEGH

### PHOTOGRAPHS BY DEBBIE PATTERSON

## LORENZ BOOKS
NEW YORK • LONDON • SYDNEY • BATH

For Ann
The ultimate lavender bag

First published in 1996 by Lorenz Books

Lorenz Books is an imprint of
Anness Publishing Inc.
27 West 20th Street
New York, NY 10011

ISBN 1 85967 206 X

*Publisher:* Joanna Lorenz
*Project Editor:* Joanne Rippin
*Designer:* Nigel Partridge
*Photographer and stylist:* Debbie Patterson
*Illustrator:* Anna Koska

Printed and bound in Singapore

*Picture Credits:*
The Bridgeman Art Library: p18;
Bruce Coleman Ltd: p. 8 (Herbert Kranawetter), p. 20 (C. Martin Pampaloni);
The Garden Picture Library: p. 16, p. 19, p. 28 (left & right), p. 32, p. 33, p. 35 (left & right);
Clive Nichols: p. 34; Visual Arts Library: p. 10.

# CONTENTS

# INTRODUCTION

**P**rized down the centuries for its perfume, medicinal properties and rich violet hues, lavender has been the darling of all herbs since time began. Among its many qualities, it is thought to calm irritable children and relieve insomnia, anxiety and depression – in other words, to create a wonderful sense of well-being. Certainly, the past few months spent working with lavender for this book have been most pleasurable, and never before has work been such a joy. Whether it was the lavender working its magic on me or because its color, perfume and form make it such a versatile and pleasurable material to use, I will never know. But I hope I have been able to pass that pleasure onto others in the ideas and projects throughout the book.

For me, lavender has particular poignancy. It takes me back to my school days in Devon where lavender grows in rich, abundant hedges in front of almost every garden. Bewitched by its perfume as I walked through the Devon country lanes, I was never able to resist picking just a few spikes to take home. I used to lay the flower heads on a tray to dry, then make a lavender bag for my mother – one each year. Those lavender bags are long lost – a casualty of many house moves – but there was no shortage of new ideas for this book, together with endless other uses for lavender.

One aim of this book was to make everything very doable, bearing in mind that often our lifestyles leave little space for time-consuming handicrafts. The other aim was not only to acknowledge lavender's rich and respected past, but also to give it a future with a fresh new look. Lavender's association with Victorian England is wonderfully romantic, but its sculpturally spiky form, intoxicating perfume and varied shades have now brought its potential far beyond the confines of simply scenting Grandma's linen chest.

*ABOVE: Collecting lavender from the quiltlike fields of England's last remaining commercial lavender farm in Norfolk.*

*RIGHT: As the sun sets over a field of lavender, the wonderful perfume scents the warm, summer evening air.*

# CHAPTER ONE

# HISTORY AND FOLKLORE

STOECHAS IS AN HERB WITH SLENDER TWIGGES

HAVEING YE HAIRE LIKE TYME, BUT YET LONGER LEAVED

AND SHARP IN YE TASTE AND SOMEWHAT BITTERISH.

*DIOSCORIDES, ABOUT AD 60*

*ABOVE: White lavender is a beautiful foil to the purple varieties.*
*LEFT: Native to the countries of the Mediterranean, lavender has
grown alongside olive trees for centuries.*

*ABOVE: Lavender helped to save the city of Jerusalem from destruction when used by Judith to stupefy the army commander, Holofernes.*

Lavender's glorious hues and beguiling aromatic perfume have ensured it a place in the hearts of men and women almost since time began. In the course of this long-lived love affair, all sorts of properties, both real and imaginary, have been attributed to it.

As well as for its unmistakable perfume, lavender has been recognized since Roman times for its healing and antiseptic qualities, its ability to deter insects, and for washing. There are many references in the Bible to the high price of lavender, using its ancient name of spikenard. In the gospel of St. Luke, the writer reports: "Then took Mary a pound of ointment of spikenard, very costly, and anointed the feet of Jesus, and wiped his feet with her hair: and the house was filled with the odor of the ointment."

Over the centuries, biblical references and folklore became entwined. It was believed that Adam and Eve took lavender with them when they were banished from the Garden of Eden. According to legend, it was not until much later that lavender received its distinctive perfume, bestowed upon it by Mary when she laid the baby Jesus' clothes on a bush to dry.

It was perhaps because of the Virgin's saintly touch that lavender came to be regarded as a safeguard against evil. Traditionally, a cross made from lavender was hung over the door for protection. In some respects, to our ancestors' minds, lavender really did ward off evil in that it appeared to guard against disease. During the Great Plague in London in the seventeenth century, it was suggested that a bunch of lavender tied to each wrist would protect against infection. It is known that the grave-robbers, who plundered plague victims' personal belongings, used to wash in Four Thieves Vinegar, which contained lavender. Although the thieves must have come into contact with the infection more than most people, they rarely contracted the disease. In sixteenth-century France, too, lavender was considered an effective and reliable protection against infection. For example, glove-makers, who were licensed to perfume their wares with lavender, escaped cholera at that time.

Nowadays, rather than its antitoxic qualities, lavender is associated with love. Certainly, in folklore, the aroma of lavender seemed to promote an almost drunken stupor in some hapless males. In one of the apocryphal books of the Bible, Judith anointed herself with perfumes including lavender before seducing Holofernes, the enemy commander. Once he was under her heavenly scented influence, she murdered him and saved the city of Jerusalem.

By Tudor times, lavender seemed to have established a hot line to Cupid. If a maiden wanted to know the identity of her true love, she would sip a brew of lavender on St. Luke's day while murmuring:

*St. Luke, St. Luke, be kind to me,*
*In my dreams, let me my true love see.*

Alpine girls tucked lavender under their lovers' pillows, hoping to turn their thoughts to romance, and once married, newlyweds would put bunches of dried lavender under their mattresses to ensure marital passion.

# BENEFICIAL LAVENDER

STOECHAS ... OPENETH THE STOPPINGS OF THE LIVER, THE LUNGS, THE MILT, THE MOTHER, THE BLADDER
AND IN ONE WORD ALL INWARD PARTS, CLENSING AND DRIVING FORTH ALL EVILL AND CURRUPT HUMOURS.
*THE HERBALL, JOHN GERARD, 1597*

For centuries, the herbs of the countryside were the people's medicine chest, and the healing qualities of lavender have always given it a leading role. The first record of its remedial properties dates back to AD 77 when the Greek Dioscorides, a military doctor, wrote, "Ye decoction of it … is good for ye griefs in ye thorax." About the same time, a Roman, Pliny the Elder, declared that lavender helped the pains of those who were bereft, those with menstrual problems, upset stomachs, kidney disorders, jaundice and dropsy. He also noted that it eased insect bites. The Roman soldiers were so impressed with its healing qualities that they took it with them on their campaigns to dress their war wounds.

Later, in the Middle Ages, it was the monks and nuns who nurtured herbs, using them to make medicines. An abbess from Mainz, Hildegarde, noted in the twelfth century, what the Romans knew centuries before, that oil of lavender was effective in treating head lice; a method that was still being used in 1874 on children in Provence. During the sixteenth century Queen Elizabeth I of England was a devotee. She drank copious cups of lavender tea to treat her frequent migraine headaches.

During the seventeenth century, lavender secured its place in the herbals as pretty much a cure-all, relieving headaches, calming nerves, healing acne, and soothing insect stings and "the bitings of serpents, mad-dogs and other venomous creatures."

By the nineteenth century, lavender appeared in the London Pharmacopeia as an ingredient of palsy drops, which supposedly remedied "falling sickness, cold distempers of the head, womb, stomach and nerves against apoplexy, palsy, convulsions, migrim, vertigo, loss of memory, dimness of sight, melancholy, swooning fits, acne and barreness in women."

More recently, during the First World War, modern antiseptics were in such short supply that the public were asked to gather garden lavender so the oil could be used together with sphagnum moss to dress war wounds.

*LEFT: Herbalists and pharmacists have been using lavender remedies since ancient times.*

*ABOVE: Lavender has been grown domestically for centuries, and used for home remedies.*

Lavender is still used in herbal remedies. Cushions filled with dried lavender can help to induce sleep and ease stress or depression. It can be brewed into a tea, which is then either drunk, used to make compresses for dressing wounds or for applying to the forehead to relieve congestion of the sinuses, headaches, hangovers, tiredness, tension and exhaustion.

Although herbal remedies are natural, they can be dangerous if used incorrectly, so it is best to take lavender internally only in the form of a weak tea, unless you are being treated by a registered herbalist.

### TO MAKE A COMPRESS
Soak a clean cloth in a hot infusion of lavender and use immediately.

### TO MAKE AN INFUSION OR TEA
Pour boiling water into a cup, let it cool for 30 seconds, then add a teaspoonful of fresh or dried lavender. Cover and leave to steep for ten minutes, stirring occasionally. Strain and drink lukewarm.

The antiseptic qualities of a weak infusion of lavender tea help to cleanse the system and to relieve headaches and stomach upsets. Sweeten it with a little honey if you prefer.

# AROMATHERAPY

LAVENDER ... IS NOT ONLY SWEET OF SMELL, AND THEREFORE COMFORTABLE TO THE BRAINE,
BUT ALSO GOOD FOR THE PALSIE AND ALL OTHER INFIRMITIES.

*HAVEN OF HEALTH, THOMAS COGHAM, 1584*

Although the word *aromatherapy* is a new one, first appearing in the 1920s in an article by chemist René-Maurice Gattefosse, the practice of it goes back many thousands of years. The Greek physician Theophrastus, who lived during the third century BC, wrote about the healing qualities of scent in his book *Concerning Odours.* The effect of aromas was obviously recognized from early times. Lavender was used for strewing, to sweeten the air, fumigate sick areas and in incense for religious ceremonies. Contemporary aromatherapists believe that odors can affect the chemical balances in the body, which could account for the mood-changing properties of aromatic herbs such as lavender.

Lavender oil earned itself a special status in modern aromatherapy, ever since Gattefosse treated a gangrenous laboratory burn on his hand with pure lavender oil and it healed remarkably quickly. He had previously noticed that severe war wounds could become infected and the poison enter the bloodstream, yet when treated with lavender oil, the poisons were detoxified and the wounds themselves healed remarkably quickly, making for a rapid overall recovery.

Aromatherapy depends on using essential oils, extracted by distillation. This is not easy to accomplish successfully at home, so most people prefer to buy them. Pure lavender oil is expensive, but it is not worth being tempted by any offered at lower prices. This is often an indication that the oil has been blended with other oils, which are not as effective in aromatherapy. It is best, therefore, to buy bottles that are marked "Pure Lavender Oil" from reputable suppliers.

### HOW TO USE ESSENTIAL LAVENDER OIL

There are many beneficial ways to use lavender oil, but like all essential oils, it is highly concentrated and should be treated with respect. Never take it internally, and never use it to treat children under 18 months old.

### In a burner

Scent the air with a romantically aromatic fragrance by burning lavender oil. Wonderful both inside or out at any time of the year, it is particularly beneficial in the summer, since it also repels insects. It relaxes the mind and relieves headaches too.

You can buy specially made porcelain burners. The top consists of a shallow bowl and under this there is a compartment to take a small candle. Put 1 tbsp warm water on to the bowl and add a few drops of the essential oil.

Light the candle, then sit back and enjoy the perfume. You will need to top up the water regularly so the bowl does not burn dry. Burners should never be left burning unattended, should never be left in a child's room and should never be left burning after you go to sleep.

### In the bath

A lavender bath is deeply relaxing, mildly antiseptic and helps to heal tiny cuts and scratches,

*BELOW: Lavender, mixed with oil for massage, releases an aroma which will help ease stress headaches and promote calm and restful sleep. It also helps muscular aches and pains. Warm the oil slightly before you begin, to release to scent.*

bites or swellings. It is also a thoroughly enjoyable way to end any day, whether you have had a hot summer ramble along country lanes or a stressful day at work.

Add five to ten drops of lavender oil to a warm bath, then lie back and luxuriate!

### For massage

Lavender oil blended with a base massage oil such as almond oil, sunflower oil or olive oil can be great for relaxing and de-stressing. Blend it in the proportion of two to three drops of essential lavender oil to 1 tsp of base oil. For larger quantities, use 20–60 drops of lavender to 7 tbsp base oil.

### As an inhalation

To clear a stuffy nose, or to help to clear skin blemishes and acne, make a facial steam bath.

Add five to eight drops of essential lavender oil to a bowl of hot, steaming water. Lean over the bowl with a clean towel covering your head and the bowl and gently inhale.

### FIRST AID WITH LAVENDER OIL

You can also use neat lavender oil drops as an antiseptic, to help to heal cuts and grazes, for inflammation including those from burns, boils, acne, dermatitis and eczema; to soothe

*Lavender oil burned in a special burner creates an evocative ambience while repelling insects.*

sunstroke, insect and animal bites; and to lift the spirits. Here are some of the ways in which lavender can be used for first aid.

### Acne

Blend two drops of pure lavender oil into your normal unscented moisturizer to help to heal stubborn blemishes and pimples.

### Burns

A drop of lavender oil on superficial burns or scalds will help to relieve the pain and make for a quick recovery.

### Colds

Add a few drops of lavender oil to a warm relaxing bath to help to eliminate the toxins. When you get out, you could dab a drop of

lavender oil under each nostril. The fumes can help to clear mucus.

### Congestion

Relieve a congested nose by putting a few drops of essential lavender oil on your handkerchief to inhale when needed during the day. At night, you could put the handkerchief on your pillow by your nose or use a lavender sleep pillow (see below), which will also decongest your nose as you sleep.

### Headaches

Dab a drop of lavender oil on each temple to help relieve migraine and other headaches.

### Insect bites

Take the sting out of bites with a drop of essential lavender oil.

### Sleeplessness

Make up a lavender pillow to lay on your pillow next to your nose as you drift off to sleep. The aroma will relax you, inducing drowsiness.

### Sunburn

Add a few drops of lavender oil to still mineral water, and use an atomizer to spritz it onto sore skin.

# THE ANCIENTS

━━ ❧❀❧ ━━

MY SWEETHEART, MY BRIDE IS A SECRET GARDEN, A WALLED GARDEN,

A PRIVATE SPRING ... THERE IS NO LACK OF HENNA AND NARD.

*SONG OF SOLOMON, ABOUT 900 BC*

Precious, aromatic lavender has been highly valued since ancient times. The Egyptians learned how to make intoxicating perfumes that almost certainly included lavender. When Tutankhamun's tomb was opened in 1922, some 3,000 years after it had been sealed, urns were found, filled with unguent that still retained traces of lavender fragrance. In those days, this valued unguent would probably have been used only by royal families or the high priests who dispensed them.

Women have always known about the power of perfume in seduction. The Queen of Sheba, trying to close a deal with King Solomon, offered gifts of frankincense, myrrh and spikenard. And Cleopatra seduced both Julius Caesar and Mark Antony with the help of perfumes including lavender.

Scenting the body was certainly not the sole prerogative of women in those days. Wealthy men in Ancient Egyptian times used to put solid cones of unguent on their heads, and as these slowly melted, they would cover their bodies with the precious heady perfumes. The Greek philosopher Diogenes in the third century BC preferred to start at the bottom, anointing his feet, rather than his head, with perfume. "When you anoint your head with perfume, it flies away in the air, and birds only get benefit of it," he reasoned, "whilst if I rub it on my lower limbs it envelopes my whole body, and gratefully ascends to my nose."

The Romans were outrageously lavish with fragrances, using aromatic oils liberally to perfume their hair, bodies, clothes and beds, and of course in their famous public baths housed in magnificent buildings. Bathing became something of a ceremony, starting with first an oiling in the *unctuarium,* followed by a cold bath in the *frigidarium,* a tepid one in the *tepidarium* and a hot one in the *caldarium.* While in the hot bath, the Romans would pour warm fragrant oils over themselves, prior to a body massage with aromatic oils. Roman women bathed at home before anointing themselves with nardium, a fragrant, lavender-based compound. At night, they hung lavender next to their beds probably as much to deter the bedbugs as to entice any prospective suitors.

Lavender's many names date from ancient times: in his seventeenth-century *Herbal Simples,* Dr. Fernie noted, "By the Greeks, the name Nardus is given to Lavender, from Naards, a city of Syria near the Euphrates." Spike refers to the shape of the flowers, and sometimes lavender was known as Indian spikenard. The Romans would recognize stoechas lavender, which they named after the Islands of Stoechades, now the Iles d'Hyères, just off the coast of the French Riviera.

*LEFT: A sundial becomes a striking focal point when fringed by white lavender, then enveloped by a double line of mauve, which itself creates a boundary between two parts of the garden.*

*RIGHT: In ancient times lavender's pointed blooms inspired its early name of "spikenard".*

# OLDE ENGLAND

*LADIES FAIR, I BRING TO YOU, LAVENDER WITH SPIKES OF BLUE;*
*SWEETER PLANT WAS NEVER FOUND, GROWING ON OUR ENGLISH GROUND.*
*CARYL BATTERSBY, EARLY TWENTIETH CENTURY*

In medieval Britain, it was the monks who preserved the knowledge of herbal lore in their diligently tended physic gardens. Way back in 1301, lavender is listed among the herbs grown at Merton Abbey. This was perhaps the first hint of the role the surrounding region would play in the history of English lavender. Situated in the center of Mitcham, this whole area was, by the middle of the nineteenth century, blanketed in rolling fields of purple lavender, making it the very epicenter of English lavender oil production. This was the cradle of all the associations of lavender, England and the Victorians.

The move from physic gardens to domestic gardens really came about after King Henry VIII of England dissolved the monasteries in the sixteenth century. Lavender began to regain the same popularity it had had in Roman times, with the ladies of manor houses making their own preparations of sweet waters in their stillrooms for gifts in times of celebration. Once again, lavender was associated with cleanliness and was strewn among linens, sewn into sweet bags, used to freshen the air and mixed with beeswax to make furniture polish.

Queen Elizabeth I adored lavender, not just to ease her migraine, but as a perfume, for which she paid dearly – £40 to a distillery for

*ABOVE: An engraving depicting a street vendor selling lavender, a fairly common sight in those days, taken from* Modern London *by Richard Phillips, published in 1804.*

a single compound. This encouraged the development of lavender farms and a continued growth of lavender products. Henrietta Maria, the wife of King Charles I, brought Continental cosmetics to the English court, introducing the idea of perfuming soap with lavender oil, making potpourri and using lavender waters for washing and bathing.

Once again, lavender joined forces with Cupid. The famous nursery rhyme "Lavender blue, dilly dilly" is derived from a more bawdy version, written in 1680, where everyone is set to work:

*Some to make hay, diddle diddle*
*Some to the corn*
*Whilst you and I, diddle diddle*
*Keep the bed warm.*

It was during the seventeenth century that the great herbalists, Gerard, Parkinson and Culpeper wrote their herbals, generating considerable public interest in all herbs. Lavender sellers became part of the street scene, asking high prices for their wares, especially during the Great Plague of 1665 when it was thought to protect against the terrible disease.

But it is Victoria's long reign that is most associated with lavender. The queen was so enthusiastic about this versatile aromatic herb that she appointed Miss Sarah Sprules "Purveyor of Lavender Essence to the Queen" and would make personal visits to Miss

*RIGHT: This simple parterre of clipped box and lavender makes a focal point in a lawn.*

Sprules' lavender fields in Wallington. The queen's homes were impregnated with the aroma of lavender. It was used to wash floors and furniture, and lavender bags were slipped between the sheets in linen presses. Victoria's love of lavender made it a fashionable fragrance among English ladies throughout the land. Those who could not afford the essence would buy fresh lavender annually from the sellers in the streets, encouraged by the now famous cries, including this:

> *Come buy my lavender, sweet maids,*
> *You cannot think it dear,*
> *There must be profit in all trades,*
> *Mine comes but once a year.*
>
> *Just put one bundle to your nose,*
> *What rose can this excel;*
> *Throw it among your finest clothes,*
> *And grateful they will smell.*

In London, the lavender was sold mainly by gypsies who brought it up from the fields of Mitcham. As well as selling it fresh, they would use dried lavender to make up gifts such as muslin bags for wardrobes, and smaller ones for young women to wear in their cleavage, in hope of attracting a suitor.

Lavender was also used to repel insects, treat lice, to perfume potpourri, furniture polish and soap, and as a cure-all in the household medicine cupboard. Victorian ladies, it seemed, never grew tired of the fragrance of lavender and, sadly, this contributed to its waning popularity in the early twentieth century during which it became associated with old ladies. But as interest gradually returned to things natural in the latter half of the century, lavender has seen a another revival.

# A WORLD OF LAVENDER

IT IS THE WONDER AND JOY OF THE SOUTH IN ITS BLUE DRESS
AND ITS SCENT IS GOD'S GIFT TO EARTH.
*MAURICE MESSEGUE, 1972*

Native to Persia and the Canaries, with some species originally hailing from all around the Mediterranean, India, Nigeria, Sudan, Yemen, Saudi Arabia, Iran, Oman and Ethiopia, lavender thrives in heat and dust. It is endowed with narrow, hairy leaves and a

*BELOW: A wonderful spiky bush of lavender, growing in a Tuscan garden in Italy.*

plentiful supply of oils to protect it from drying out. It is surprising, therefore, that in Victorian times, it was Mitcham, now a London suburb of back-to-back terraces, that was the English center of lavender oil production. Its sunny south-facing, well-drained slopes were clothed in amethyst, exuding the heady fragrance that had become known as quintessentially English.

Lavender not only thrived in England's relatively damp and chilly climate, it excelled. The combination of long summer days and harsher conditions encourage the plant to make more oil. English lavender produced the finest oil and fetched up to 200 shillings a pound in 1881, while French and Dutch oils cost a mere 18 shillings. English lavender products became known the world over, largely due to old-established companies, such as Yardley's and Potter and Moore, which sold lavender waters and lavender soaps.

The lack of the endless hot sunny days of lavender's native climate has obviously never been a problem for English varieties. Way back in the seventeenth century, John Parkinson noted among his herbals that French lavender was "somewhat sweete, but nothing compared with lavender," and Mrs Leyel, founder of the Society of Herbalists, wrote in 1931 that she had "often come across fields of French Lavender in bloom, and that the scent has been poor compared with English Lavender grown under the worst conditions."

Even so, a combination of disease and the pressure of ever-increasing land values meant that suburban terraces gradually replaced the lavender fields of Mitcham, Wallington and Carshalton. The English lavender industry would have been long extinct, had it not been saved by Linn Chilvers, a nurseryman in Norfolk. In 1932, he decided to try growing lavender on a commercial scale. When he died, his trustee, Adrian Head and his wife, Ann, took an active role in the business. Ann is still a director and their son, Henry, is Managing Director, continuing the tradition by nurturing 100 acres of rolling fields of lavender for the distillation of pure English lavender oil.

It is the sun-baked slopes of Provence, around Grasse, the center of the perfume industry, that now reigns as the world's largest lavender producer. Originally brought to the area by the Romans, lavender took a liking to the southern slopes of the Alps with their well-drained soil, and began to grow wild in the region. By the turn of the twentieth century, local shepherds collected it for sale to the

*LEFT AND ABOVE: The Norfolk lavender farmhouse in all its summer glory, surrounded by blooms.*

perfumers of Grasse, but it was still not cultivated. However, the perfume houses and the French government saw that lavender could provide a means of stopping people leaving the area for the cities. With this double back-

ing, just before the First World War, they cleared the almond orchards and planted lavender in its place. Provence had staked its claim as the world's leading lavender producer.

There are now many other producers of lavender around the world, including Spain, the Netherlands, Belgium, Germany, Bulgaria, Russia, Australia, Japan, Canada and the United States.

In North America, it was the Shakers who first grew lavender commercially. This strict breakaway sect of the English Quakers set out to be self-sufficient when they arrived in New England, and developed well-maintained herb farms. These herbs and the resulting medicines made in the Shakers' own pharmacies were sold to the "outside world" in beautiful simple packaging that very often listed all the ingredients of the contents, which was unusual at the time.

Lavender was a favorite herbal ingredient for gift items as well as medicines. Backed by slick New York advertising in the last century, and respected for its honest quality, Shaker lavender produce soon found its way back to England. Even today, a few lavender items made by the remaining Shaker communities and specialist Shaker craftspeople are sold around the world.

# CHAPTER TWO

# CULTIVATION

FRENCH LEVENDER BEING A HERBE OF VERY GOOD SMELL,
AND VERY USUAL IN LANGUEDOC AND PROVENCE,
DOTH CRAVE TO BE DILIGENTLY TILLED IN A FAT GROUND
AND LYING OPEN TO THE SUNNE.

*THE COUNTRIE FARM, RICHARD SURFLEET, 1600*

*ABOVE: Lavender in full bloom, just ready for harvest.*
*LEFT: While lavender is mostly cut by machine, some is harvested
by hand and transported to the distillery in wooden boxes.*

*ABOVE: Lavender fields in bloom emit a fragrance that is as beguiling as the rich color.*

Few people could not be seduced by the sight and fragrance of a lavender field in full bloom. The bushes, laid out in rows like a magnificent amethyst quilt enveloping the land, provide a memorable experience, made all the more powerful by the intoxicating aroma and the persistent humming of bees.

Lavender was not always cultivated like this. For a long time, especially in the south of France, it was not cultivated at all, rather it was gathered from the hills by shepherds and local people who supplied the perfumers of Grasse. When the French did begin to cultivate commercially, they followed the English pattern of planting the bushes individually with

*BELOW: Lines of different varieties of lavender make a rich textural pattern.*

ample space around each one. It was not until the mid-1950s, in anticipation of mechanical cutters, that the bushes were planted in the neat rows we now associate with lavender fields. Nine years later the machines began to ease the toil of harvesting.

However, in Britain, lavender had been cultivated on a much smaller scale for centuries, originally by monks in their well-organized physic gardens for use in various remedies and medicines. Each variety of herb usually had its own separate bed for ease of identification, and this was probably the inspiration for the knot gardens and parterres that first became popular during the time of Elizabeth I.

Partly because lavender is native to the hot, dry climate of the Mediterranean and Middle East, it has never had trouble settling in America, and has become the mainstay of the traditional English cottage garden. As well as single bushes, glorious indigo hedges of lavender are a common sight in many parts.

One of the reasons lavender is so successful in such differing climates is that it hybridizes very readily, and so there is usually a variety that can adapt to suit the local environment. Over the centuries, this has caused much argument among the lavender *cognoscenti,* and even nurserymen have been known to get a variety wrong. To add to the confusion, lavender is sometimes given national names such as English, French, Dutch or Spanish lavender, none of which are actual varieties, merely names given to the variety most commonly grown in the relevant country.

In Britain, there are two main types of lavender that are frost-hardy and happy to be here, and within those two types, there are endless hybrids. The most common garden type is *Lavandula angustifolia,* which used to be sometimes known as *L. vera* or *L. officinalis.* It is a stocky, sweet-smelling plant, carrying just

one flower spike on each stem. The other main type is *Lavandula* x *intermedia,* which is a cross between *Lavandula angustifolia* and *Lavandula latifolia,* (a narrow-leaved, shrubby plant that grows wild in the Mediterranean). *Lavandula* x *intermedia* has the frost-hardiness of *L. angustifolia* combined with the camphorous perfume and axial shoots of *L. latifolia.*

*ABOVE: While French lavender grows on the slopes of the Alps, English lavender is now cultivated on flatter fields. However, both have the vital well-drained soil needed for lavender cultivation.*

Another type that is becoming increasingly popular in America is *L. stoechas.* The varieties in this group are easy to recognize since they carry flamboyant, butterfly-like, colored bracts on top of the flowers. Abundant in the Iles d'Hyères off the French Riviera, this type is sometimes known as French lavender and is almost certainly a type the Romans would have recognized. Most of this group is not frost-hardy, and includes several lavenders that have pretty fernlike leaves.

# LAVENDER DIRECTORY

Lavender blue dilly, dilly, Lavender green,
When I am king, dilly dilly, You'll be my queen.
*Traditional nursery rhyme*

We expect lavender to span a color range from palest lilac to deepest indigo. But when we start a love affair with it, we find there are green, pink and even white varieties too. Blooms can be tall and spiky or stocky and tightly packed. Leaves can be long and slim or fuller and ferny.

Lavender falls into several types: *Lavandula latifolia,* a narrow-leaved lavender that grows wild in the Mediterranean; *L. angustifolia,* which is stockier and has a fuller flower; and *L. x intermedia,* which is a cross between the two, and is sometimes called lavandin. Another group, *L. stoechas,* has butterfly bracts on top of the flowers, and is sometimes known as French or Spanish lavender. Some varieties in this type have decorative fernlike leaves. A fourth group is *L. Ptero stoechas,* which is not frost-hardy, and sometimes temperamental.

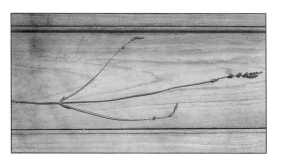

*ABOVE: Lavandula latifolia*

### L. Latifolia types

*L. LATIFOLIA* is rarely seen in damp climates because it is prone to disease, but flourishes in Mediterranean-climate gardens. Its strong fragrance has formed the basis of the Spanish spike oil industry, being used extensively to perfume furniture wax, air fresheners and polishes.
*L. LATIFOLIA X LANATA* 'SAWYERS': Large, tapered blooms make this a glorious garden plant.

### L. Angustifolia types

*L. ANGUSTIFOLIA* 'IMPERIAL GEM': Similar to 'Hidcote,' which is often thought of as English, it is a mainstay of cottage gardens. Popular for its abundant indigo blooms.
*L. ANGUSTIFOLIA* 'NANA ALBA': Also known as dwarf white or baby white. A different lavender with white blooms on a compact bush that grows only 12 in high.
*L. ANGUSTIFOLIA* 'ROSEA': A delightful pink-flowered lavender.

### L. Intermedia types (Lavandin)

*L. X INTERMEDIA* 'GRAPPENHILL': Traditional English garden lavender with blue purple flowers, both on leading and axial shoots.
*L. X INTERMEDIA* 'GROSSO': A wonderful hybrid with an attractive, large, fat flower named after M. Pierre Grosso.

*BELOW: Lavandula latifolia x lanata 'Sawyers'*

*BELOW: Lavandula angustifolia 'Imperial Gem'*

*BELOW: Lavandula angustifolia 'Nana Alba'*

*ABOVE: Lavandula angustifolia* 'Miss Katherine'

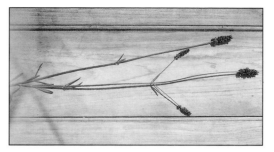

*ABOVE: Lavandula* x *intermedia* 'Hidcote Giant'

*ABOVE: Lavandula stoechas viridis*

*ABOVE: Lavandula* x *intermedia* 'Grappenhill'

*ABOVE: Lavandula stoechas*

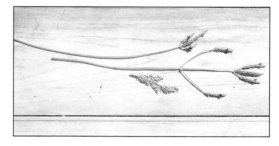

*ABOVE: Lavandula pinnata*

*ABOVE: Lavandula* x *intermedia* 'Grosso'

*ABOVE: Lavandula stoechas pedunculata*

*ABOVE: Lavandula canariensis*

*L. X INTERMEDIA* 'HIDCOTE GIANT': Heavily scented, this large shrub has generous compact flowers, making it excellent for dried arrangements.

### Stoechas types
*L. STOECHAS*: A delightful compact lavender which exhibits the distinctive petal-like bracts on top of the flower. This plant is often known as French lavender.

*L. STOECHAS PEDUNCULATA*: This is a somewhat taller variety of the *stoechas* which also has larger top bracts.

*L. STOECHAS VIRIDIS*: The small bracts on this beautiful green lavender immediately betray its *stoechas* heritage.

### L. Ptero Stoechas types
*L. PINNATA*: A delicate-looking, half-hardy plant with small blooms, carrying three blooms on the leading stem and having lower axial shoots. It also has distinctive dentata-style ferny leaves.

*L. CANARIENSIS*: This is similar to *L. pinnata,* only carrying just one bloom on the leading stem, and having axial shoots.

# SOIL AND CLIMATE

*BEST AMONG ALL GOOD PLANTS FOR HOT SANDY SOILS ARE THE EVER BLESSED LAVENDER AND ROSEMARY.*
*GERTRUDE JEKYLL, 1900*

Lavender is an extraordinarily versatile and resilient plant. Hailing from the heat and dust of the sun-drenched countries around the Mediterranean, and even the desert regions of Saudi Arabia, the Yemen and Ethiopia, it is truly surprising that it is also happy living in the damp northern climes of the Pacific Northwest and the Midwest. The reason is that not all varieties are hardy in all climates.

*ABOVE: Lavenders in lilac, indigo and white, planted informally and allowed to grow freely, create a natural-looking environment, almost as if they were in the wild.*

*LEFT: White lavender with indigo 'Hidcote' lavender makes a striking combination.*

While some, native to hotter climes, cannot tolerate any frost, others, such as *Lavandula angustifolia,* are hardy and will survive through zone 5 or to below 0°F.

Whether lavender grows in the heat of the desert or the damp chill of the northern Pacific coast, it does need light soil – preferably sand

or gravel in a dry, open sunny position with good drainage so the roots do not get water-logged in winter. Generally, lavender is not keen on acid soils, preferring alkaline ones. If your soil is acid, use lots of garden lime, and add a top dressing annually. If you live in a very heavy clay area, dig a deep hole, line it

*ABOVE: Hot and dry or chilly and damp, lavender can thrive in a surprisingly wide variety of climates without too much attention.*

with gravel to help the drainage and then add sand to the soil when planting. A little manure added when planting will help to establish the

shrubs, but do not add too much as this will stimulate leaf growth rather than creating more flower heads and will also dissipate the fragrance. Not at all difficult to grow, lavender hardly needs any fertilizer; too much nourishment would simply go into growing more leaves, which is not the desired outcome.

# NURTURING LAVENDER

*LAVENDER SPIKE HATH MANY STIFF BRANCHES OF A WOODY SUBSTANCE ... THE FLOURES
GROW AT THE TOP OF THE BRANCHES, SPIKE FASHION, OF A BLEW COLOR.*
*THE HERBALL, JOHN GERARD, 1597*

It is not difficult to propagate lavender. But since it naturally hybridizes so readily, it does have some surprising characteristics. Some hybrids are called "mules" and will never produce their own seed, so these have to be propagated by taking cuttings.

### TAKING CUTTINGS

In spring or autumn, choose a young shoot about 2 in long, and pull it downward sharply,

so it comes away with a "heel." Dip the heel end of the cutting into a hormone rooting compound and plant it in light, sandy soil mix. Keep it moist and protect it from frost. Spring cuttings root quickest – in about six weeks.

### SOWING FROM SEED

Even if you do have a plant that produces seed, you may find its offspring a little unpredictable. Lavender hybridizes so readily that a single bush can produce shrubs of quite different sizes carrying different flowers. Added to this, the seed is not very reliable, so you need to plant plenty of it in April, then prick off the resulting seedlings into their own pots once they are established.

### BUYING PLANTS

By far the most reliable and easiest form of cultivation is to buy the young plants, which are available from garden centers or growers. Make sure you know what you are getting by purchasing either well-known varieties of

*LEFT: Taking cuttings is an easy, efficient and probably the most reliable way to propagate lavender. The woody cutting on the left is a hardwood cutting, the soft leafy one on the right is a softwood cutting.*

*ABOVE: Seed can be collected by tying a bag around the heads of ripened lavender to catch it when it falls. It can also be bought from seed companies by mail.*

lavender or buying when the bush is already in bloom.

### PLANTING OUT

Young plants can be planted out once the frosts are over. Traditionally, growers allow 2 ft between each plant, though if you are planning a hedge, plant them closer, 12–18 in apart. Some experts say that lavender should not be allowed to flower in its first year to encourage a strong, bushy growth. It will produce a full complement of blooms from the second year onwards, and will reach full size

by the fifth year. To help prevent the bush from becoming straggly, at the end of August cut the flower stems right down where they leave the bush. The lavender should be pruned hard in March to encourage a good growth in the summer.

*ABOVE: Young plants can be bought at various stages from growers and garden centers.*

*LEFT: Once the frosts are over, the lavender plants are ready to be planted out.*

# LAVENDER GARDENS

*... AN ARBER FAYRE TO PARADISE, RIGHT WELL COMPARABLE, SET ALL ABOUT WITH FLOWERS FRAGRANT.*

*HAWES, 1554*

The most glorious gardens stimulate all five senses, and many would say that fragrance comes a very close second to the look of the garden. The very word paradise is said to come from *pairidaeza,* which was the name for enclosed scented gardens in Persia 2,000 years ago. Since some varieties of lavender are native to Persia, it is doubtless that lavender took a starring role in those ancient *pairidaezas.*

Lavender is seeing a resurgence along with cottage-style gardens, many of which have at least one lavender bush in their borders, but there is so much more you can do with this richly fragranced shrub.

If the garden is large enough, you could plant swaths of it, letting it colonize areas of the garden that might otherwise have been a touch scrubby. Its indigo hues in summer and

*RIGHT: Swaths of lavender release a heady scent, creating an evocative, memorable ambience for summer days in the garden.*

*BELOW: Lavender and roses make perfect planting companions, offering delightful combinations of scent and color. Low-growing lavender can also be used as decorative ground cover for what can be a leggy shrub.*

*LEFT: Rows of indigo lavender bushes make spectacular borders for this charming well-stocked herb garden in France.*

*RIGHT: Hedges of lavender release their sweet fragrance as visitors make their way down this English country cottage pathway.*

*BELOW: The distinctive butterfly-like bracts of* Lavandula stoechas *make a delightful sight in a cottage border.* L. stoechas, *sometimes known as French or Spanish lavender, may not be hardy to frost, so it is wise to plant it in a decorative pot like this mosaic one so it can be moved and over-wintered under glass.*

the gentle gray green of the leaves in winter will provide a year-round blanket of color. In summer too, its pungent aroma will not only attract gently humming bees and butterflies, but repel less welcome guests such as some slugs, flies and millipedes.

Another delightful way of using lavender is to take inspiration from the gardens of yore when it was used in a more formal, architectural way. The English Tudors made intricate knot gardens, creating elaborate patterns of low-clipped box hedges with each section either planted with herbs or filled with colored gravel. By the seventeenth century, these knot gardens were set together in geometric arrangements that were known as parterres. Nowadays, a mini knot garden or even a parterre, perhaps planted with different varieties of lavender, could make a spectacular feature within the larger framework of the whole garden.

As well as being used within the framework of multi-shrub mini hedging, lavender makes a marvelous indigo hedge itself. Use it as a border for pathways or large flower beds, or let it tumble over a low wall, for example, to create a spectacular boundary to the front garden, striking in both country and city.

# HARVESTING AND DISTILLING

*... AND AS FOR THE TIME OF GATHERING FLOWERS, LET IT BE WHEN THE SUN SHINES UPON THEM,*
*SO THEY MAY BE DRY, FOR IF YOU GATHER WHEN THEY BE WET OR DEWY, THEY WILL NOT KEEP.*
*CULPEPER*

A year's work nurturing lavender in the fields all hangs in the balance on the day for harvesting. However carefully the bushes have been planted, pruned and nurtured as

*BELOW: Hand sickles were the traditional tool for cutting lavender. They are still used for small sampling jobs and for the lavender that will be sold in bunches. But the main harvest for distilling is now brought in mechanically.*

they bloom and produce their precious oil, all can go to waste if the conditions are not right on the day of harvesting. It is not simply a decision based on how ripe the flowers are. When they are ready for harvesting, the weather must be set fair because if it turns damp or rainy even during the harvest, the results will be disappointing.

Gauging the time to commence harvesting is the most critical decision of the year. The flowers have to be fully developed so they contain the maximum amount of oil, but not over-mature when the florets start to drop. A dry spell around the end of July and beginning of August is usually the best time, depending on the weather. Rain is disastrous at harvest time because any damp on the cut lavender will make the florets turn brown and then drop off. Even under the best weather conditions, the lavender has to be gathered quickly and taken straight to the distillation stills as fast as possible before any of the oils have the chance to dry out.

The best time to cut lavender is in the early morning or evening of a fine day, as the mid-day heat encourages it to release some of its precious scent. Cut the stalks with sharp pruning shears, and take the lavender inside immediately, away from the hot sun.

*ABOVE: The lavender is tied into bunches as it is cut, and laid on the now-shorn bushes.*

Most commercial lavender goes to the distillery. The cut lavender is loaded into the still, steam is passed through, vaporizing the oil, which then cools to become a clear gold liquid. In the hour this takes, 350 lb of lavender produces just 18 fl oz of oil, which must be left to mature for a year.

ABOVE: Lavender destined for the distillery does not need to be tied into bunches, so it is loosely bagged up on the machine and taken straight to the stills. There, it is emptied onto the distillery floor and then shoveled into the still.

LEFT: The original old wooden crates are still used by Norfolk Lavender for transporting by truck back to the warehouse.

ABOVE: These old copper stills have been distilling lavender oil since 1874, producing a fragrance that experienced perfumers can distinguish from that of oil which is distilled in the more modern stainless steel stills.

# BUNCHING AND DRYING

Nothing quite captures the essence of summer so well as dried lavender, which continues to release its fragrance for at least 8 months and, after an initial fading, retains a soft indigo hue. It can be dried in two forms:

*BELOW: Lavender destined for drying needs to be bunched up as it is cut.*

in bunches for dried flower arrangements, and as florets for filling sachets, cushions, linen bags, wallhangings and even oven gloves.

Commercially, the bunches are tied to a special drying rack that is hoisted up on to the wall of the drying barn. Loose lavender is left in its sacks and warm air is passed through it for two to three days. The florets are then separated from the stalks and sieved several times in a special sifter until only the flowers remain.

At home, cut lavender blooms for dried arrangements before the florets open; cut those for potpourri a little later when the oil, and therefore the fragrance, has had time to develop. Make up the lavender into small bunches as you cut it, then secure with elastic bands which will tighten as the lavender shrinks during the drying process. The bunches then need to be hung up in a dry place with plenty of air circulating.

Lavender smells so fabulous and the bunches look so pretty, you can use them to decorate the house. Attached to the bottom of the spindles, hanging into the stairwell all the way up the stairs, for example, they will get plenty of air movement and be safely protected from knocks. If you wish, tie bunches with decorative twine, ribbon or even scraps of fabric. Drying loose lavender is even easier. Simply

*ABOVE: Large bunches of lavender are dried commercially on frames hoisted on to the walls of the drying barn. At home, they can be on strings, or simply hung on any wall where there is plenty of air circulation.*

spread it out on trays in a well-aired room. Once the lavender is completely dry, it is easy to strip the florets from the stalks by gently rubbing them between your fingers.

*ABOVE: Rows of lavender bunches hung up to dry always look decorative, even when held together with a rubber band. The bunches should be well spaced to ensure good air circulation which speeds the drying process.*

# CHAPTER THREE

# LAVENDER AND LINEN

LET'S GO TO THAT HOUSE, FOR THE LINEN LOOKS WHITE AND SMELLS OF LAVENDER, AND I LONG TO LIE IN A PAIR OF SHEETS THAT SMELL SO.

*THE COMPLEAT ANGLER, IZAAK WALTON, 1653*

*ABOVE: Lavender is often used to scent pretty bags such as these.*
*LEFT: A lavender field in full bloom, just minutes before harvest begins, is a breathtaking sight.*

The association between lavender and wash day has been a long and often romantic one. Its very name comes from the Latin *lavare*, "to wash," and over the centuries this came to mean clothes and household linens as well as bathing. Lavender's exquisite aromatic smell was its obvious attraction. When dried and strewn in the linen cupboard, it also had the advantage of deterring insects and moths that could spoil the clothes.

Constance Isherwood, in her turn-of-the-twentieth century brochure on the lavender industry, boasted:

> *Velvet gown and dainty fur,*
> *should be laid in lavender,*
> *For its sweetness drives away*
> *Fretting moths of silver grey.*

To have one's clothes stored or "laid up" in lavender meant that they were being given special care … and indeed, by all reports, it was a costly business. In 1592, during Shakespeare's lifetime, Greene noted of one cash-strapped man: "The poore gentleman paies so deere for the lavender it is laid up in, that if it laies long at the broker's house, he seems to buy his apparel twice."

More generally, clothes were strewn with

*ABOVE: In warm climates, what better way to dry laundry than draped over lavender?*

lavender to lend a personal fragrance to the owner. Brides would sprinkle dried lavender in their trousseaux, and William Langham, in the *Garden of Health* in 1579, suggested that lavender be boiled in water, then, he advised,

"Wet thy shirt in it, dry it again and wear it." And by the time of the London Cries, the lavender sellers exhorted young ladies to:

> *Come buy my sweet lavender, sweet maids…*
> *throw it among your finest clothes.*
> *And grateful they will smell.*

In Italy, and among the Shaker communities in the United States in the last century, clothes and linens were laid on lavender bushes in the hot sun to absorb the fragrance.

Before the seventeenth century, lavender was used in the chests of drawers and linen presses of the more wealthy homes to overcome the rancid smell of soap which was not yet perfumed. Nowadays, it is a wonderful way of lending a fresh smell to all household linens and clothes.

Traditionally, young girls and women wove stems of lavender into lavender bottles or sewed sachets to fill with dried lavender flowers. This is still a delightful thing to do, and since these "sweet bags" do not need to be large, they are quick to make. Also, as only scraps are needed, they can be made from extravagantly rich fabrics, such as silks and velvets, satin and lace. Appliqué or embroider them; make them in heart shapes, squares,

triangles or rectangles; make them fancy, or make them "country" simple to suit your individual style. Sachets can be made to lay among the linens and clothes, or with ribbon or wire loops added to hang on coathangers, on the inside of cabinet doors, or even on the outside to scent the whole room.

Lavender sachets and bags are the most

*ABOVE: Lavender has long been used to scent linen. Place dried bunches in your wardrobe.*

satisfying items to make, since you really do not need a lot of lavender, and the loose dried flowers, perhaps left over from a dried arrangement or bought in bags, are perfect. You can, of course, pick the flowers from your garden

and dry them yourself, to bring the fresh scent of your own garden into the house to enjoy for the rest of the year. Although it is generally accepted that dried lavender flowers will continue being fragrant for only eight months or so, a gentle squeeze and a shake every so often will release the perfume, which keeps the linen sweet for much longer.

# SHAKER SACHETS

These delightful country-style sachets are Shaker-inspired, being made in natural cotton checked fabrics and decorated with sprigs of dried lavender. The heart was a favorite Shaker motif, symbolic of their saying: "Hands to work and heart to God." Attached to wires, they can be hung on the inside of a cabinet to scent its contents.

*MATERIALS*
*paper and pencil for template*
*scissors*
*fabric, at least 20 x 10 in*
*pins, needle and sewing thread*
*loose, dried lavender*
*wire*
*6 sprigs dried lavender*
*raffia or ribbon to tie*

1 ❧ Trace the heart-shaped template or make one about 8 in high. Using this as a pattern, cut out two fabric hearts. With right sides facing, stitch the hearts together around the outside edge, leaving a gap of 2 in on the straight part of one side. Trim the seams to about ¼ in and clip into the seam allowance at intervals around the curves of the heart.

2 ❧ Turn the heart right side out, fill generously with loose, dried lavender and slip-stitch to close the gap. Bend both ends of a 12 in length of wire into hooks, then fit them into the seam at the top curves of the heart. Bend the wire a little more to close and shape.

3 ❧ Make two bunches of three sprigs of lavender, using wire to secure, then cross these over each other and wire them together. Tie with raffia or ribbon and stitch to the front of the heart.

# LACY LAVENDER HEART

The ribbons and lace on this exquisitely pretty, heart-shaped lavender bag lend a Victorian feel, evoking an era when the rich perfume of English lavender was the most sought after in the world.

*MATERIALS*
*paper and pencil for template*
*scissors*
*silky muslin, about 24 x 8 in*
*pins, needle and sewing thread*
*stranded embroidery thread*
*pearl button*
*loose, dried lavender*
*20 in antique lace*
*20 in very narrow satin ribbon*
*20 in ribbon for bow (preferably chiffon)*

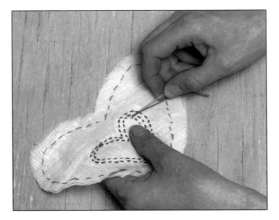

1 ⧗ Make a heart-shaped template about 6 in high. Using this as a pattern, cut out four muslin hearts and baste them in pairs so each one has a double thickness of muslin. Cut a smaller muslin heart and stitch to the front of one of the larger hearts using two strands of embroidery thread.

2 ⧗ Make another row of running stitches inside the first row. Using the same thread, sew on the pearl button, then make another row of running stitches inside the other two. With right sides facing, stitch around the edge of the two large double-thickness muslin shapes, leaving a 2 in gap along one of the straight sides.

3 ⧗ Trim the seams, then snip into the seam around the curves and snip off the bottom point. Turn the heart right side out, fill with lavender, then slip-stitch to close the gap. Slip-stitch the lace around the edge. Stitch the satin ribbon over the lower edge of the lace. Make a bow with the chiffon ribbon and stitch onto the heart.

# LAVENDER BOTTLES

Young ladies in Victorian times used to while away afternoons making lavender bottles by encasing lavender heads in their own stalks, then weaving them with ribbon. Sadly, these charming drawer and cabinet scenters are all but extinct. Although they are not difficult to make, they are fussy and time-consuming, which means they are not commercially viable. Revive the tradition by making your own, using ribbons in muted colors to complement the lavender. Each bottle uses up a fair amount of ribbon, but since the quantity depends on both the length of the lavender stalks and the width of the ribbon, it is best to buy, say, 2¼ yd and make several of these bottles.

*MATERIALS*
*9 (or any odd number) stalks freshly*
*picked lavender*
*1 yd narrow satin or rayon ribbon*

1 ※ Make a bunch of the lavender and, using the ribbon, tie their stalks together tightly at the top.

2 ※ Very carefully bend the stalks down one by one over the lavender heads, being careful not to snap them.

3 ※ Weave the ribbon in and out of the lavender stalks. When you have covered the heads, wrap the ribbon around the stalks and bind them to their ends. Cover the ends of the stalks with the ribbon, then bind back up the stalks until you reach the heads again. Tie in a knot and a bow to fasten.

# BUTTONED BAGS

The simplest ideas can often be the most effective. These miniature pillows of lavender have been decorated with rows of buttons and velvet ribbon to make elegant decorative drawer scenters.

*MATERIALS*
*scissors*
*scraps of silk, at least 12 x 8 in*
*16 in velvet ribbon, about ¾ in wide*
*6 round buttons, ⅓ in diameter*
*2 heart-shaped buttons*
*needle and sewing thread*
*loose, dried lavender*

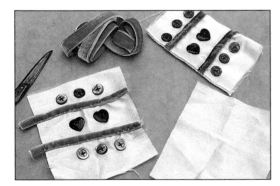

1 ✿ Cut out two pieces of silk about 5½ x 4 in and two lengths of ribbon a little longer than the width of the silk. Fold in half lengthwise and sew a little more than a third in from each end of one piece of silk. Stitch on the buttons.

2 ✿ With right sides facing, sew the two rectangles together down the long sides. Turn right side out. Use another length of ribbon to bind the bottom of the bag by folding it in half lengthwise over the end and tucking in the ends, then sewing through all the thicknesses. Fill the bag with the loose, dried lavender, making sure you don't overfill it. Bind the top in the same way as the bottom.

# LAVENDER LINEN BAG

The top of this delightful draw-string linen bag has been filled with lavender to scent its contents sweetly. A fringed edging – in this case cut from a tablecloth – has been used to trim the bottom of the bag.

*MATERIALS*
*1⅔ yd main fabric*
*1 yd fringe*
*pins, needle and sewing thread*
*1 yd x 4 in organza*
*1 yd rayon ribbon*
*2¼ yd 6 in grosgrain ribbon*
*bodkin or large safety pin*
*chenille knitting yarn*
*2 large beads*
*loose, dried lavender*

1 ⨯ From the main fabric, cut out a 9½ in circle, two rectangles measuring 20 x 16 in and two rectangles for binding measuring 10½ x 2 in. Cut the length of fringe in half. Fold the circle in half and mark the fold with pins at either side. Fold it in half the other way and mark with pins. Fold both of the larger pieces of fabric in half lengthwise and mark with pins. With right sides facing, match the pin on one piece to one of the pins on the circle. Match the pin on the other piece to the pin on the opposite side of the circle. Sandwich the fringing between the circle and the pieces with raw edges matching. Baste the pieces to the circle, then stitch, leaving the side seams open.

2 ⨯ With wrong sides facing, stitch a 4 in wide strip of organza to the top of the bag. Fold to the outside of the bag. Stitch a length of rayon ribbon over the raw edge. Repeat on the other piece of main fabric. With right sides together, stitch one of the binding strips to the top end of one side of one of the pieces of main fabric, stitching through the layer of organza where applicable. The binding should reach about halfway down the side of the main fabric. Turn over lengthwise and stitch to finish binding. Repeat on one side of the other piece of main fabric. Fill the organza channel with lavender from the open end. Bind this in the same way as before. ▶

3 ❧ Fold the whole organza channel to the inside of the bag and stitch through all layers close to the bottom edge of the organza. Make the draw-string casing by sewing another row of stitching to allow for the width of the ribbon.

4 ❧ With right sides together, stitch the side seams. Use another strip of fabric to bind the seam. Cut the grosgrain ribbon in half and, using a bodkin, thread one piece through the casing. Thread the other piece of ribbon through in the other direction.

5 ❧ Make a tassel by winding the chenille yarn around four fingers. When satisfied with the thickness, cut the chenille.

6 ❧ Take another double thickness of chenille and pass through the top of the original chenille. Pass the ends through the hole in the bead and knot tightly at the top. Trim the ends of the tassel and sew it between the two ends of ribbon.

# LITTLE LAVENDER CLOTHES HEART

A little heart of lavender is a charming way to scent the wardrobe. It can be fragile, so hang it on the inside or even the outside of the door, where it will not be crushed.

*MATERIALS*
*1 yd medium-gauge garden wire*
*raffia – preferably blue-dyed*
*1 bunch dried lavender*
*glue gun and hot wax glue*
*scissors*

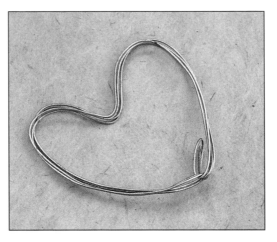

1 ☆ Fold the garden wire in half and in half again. Make a hook at one end and hook into the loop at the other end. Make a dip in the top to form a heart.

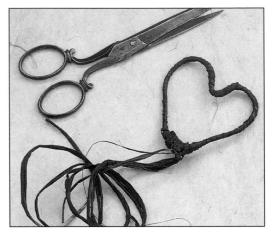

2 ☆ Bind the heart with raffia. Start at the bottom, working around the heart. Tie the ends together.

3 ☆ Starting at the dip at the top of the heart, bind three stalks of lavender to the heart with the stalks pointing inward and downward. Continue to bind the stalks in bunches of three to the heart, so that they cover the wire, working down the heart. When you reach the bottom, start at the middle of the top again and bind down toward the point. For the bottom, make a larger bunch and glue in position with the flower heads pointing upward. Trim the stalks close to the heads.

—⊱≈⊰ CHAPTER FOUR ⊱≈⊰—

# *DECORATIVE LAVENDER*

—◆≈◆—

LADIES FAIR, I BRING TO YOU
LAVENDER WITH SPIKES OF BLUE;
SWEETER PLANT WAS NEVER FOUND
GROWING ON AN ENGLISH GROUND.
*CARYL BATTERSBY IN A BUNCH OF SWEET LAVENDER,*
*CONSTANCE ISHERWOOD, 1900*

*ABOVE: Sunflowers and lavender make a perfect match.*
*LEFT: Retaining its rich purple tones, even when dried, lavender*
*makes a glorious material for arrangements around the home.*

*LEFT: As well as the much-loved blue shades, lavender comes in palest pinks and soft whites.*

*BELOW: Fresh white lavender is one of summer's rarer delights. Pick it to enjoy when fresh because it does not dry as well as the indigo varieties.*

Lavender blues, in hues from deepest indigo through amethyst, violet and hyacinth, all evoke a richness that is well documented throughout history. Purple symbolizes majesty in many cultures. Maybe it is the richness of the color that makes it so attractive, maybe it is its vast range of shades, from pink and red to blue, that means it can be mixed and matched to many other tones. Undoubtedly, purple is an evocative color, and what better way to use it than with another natural material? As well as the familiar indigo blues, there are the rarer white, pink, and even green varieties that complement the blues.

At its best fresh, lavender needs little fussing. Just bunch it and tie with a simple ribbon, or weave it into a pretty wreath or garland for a special occasion. The effort is worth it, as lavender dries readily, even when made up. The Victorians wove garlands of it around the portrait of the head of the family on celebration days. You may not wish to go that far, though a lavender wreath can be fabulous as a wall, table, or church decoration on festive days, and the dried version can serve as a souvenir afterwards.

Dried lavender, too, can make wonderful indoor decorations. Its simple, almost architectural form makes it suitable for a variety of arrangements that not only look decorative, but scent the room sweetly at the same time. But just as it was in the past, lavender by the bunch is still expensive, and because the flowers are tall and spiky-slim, the

decorations use a lot of material. The ideal situation is to have your own lavender hedge so you can cut and dry it, building up a stock of material over the summer. You use an extraordinary amount of lavender in making decorations, so if you do not grow your own, it would probably be best to adjust the arrangements a little, making smaller displays, rather than using the material too sparingly.

Try to get lavender that has densely packed florets, even though the most common variety is usually more feathery in appearance. This works just as well as the densely packed varieties but you have to use much more of it, making it very difficult to estimate the quantities required for the following designs. A bunch or even a specific number of stems can be very misleading. The best solution is to buy as much lavender as you can afford, then work out how much area it would cover by measuring the space taken up by the tips of the flower spikes. Buy a florists' foam base in a size they would easily cover. All the designs on the following pages look just as effective when they are scaled down.

*LEFT: Fresh lavender looks stunning on its own in simple containers. Fill several to make a delightful still life.*

# DETAILS THAT COUNT

Even small bunches of lavender can be used decoratively. Tie them – fresh or dried – to the backs of chairs as a scented decoration when entertaining indoors or out. As guests brush against the lavender, they will bruise the flowers, releasing the rich fragrance. Small bunches can be used decoratively in a more permanent way too. Simple bunches can be tied and attached to photograph or picture frames, hung above the bathroom mirror or as a welcome on the front door. Lavender's uncomplicated form calls for uncluttered tying. Think in terms of garden raffia, natural colored string or twine or plain narrow ribbons. They all look good.

*LEFT: Let the soldier-straight stems of lavender, in their exquisite gray-green, become part of the decoration. Here, two bunches stand guard either side of a driftwood colored picture frame. Wire the bunches together, tie with colored string, then secure them in position with a glue gun and hot wax glue.*

*RIGHT: Bunches of lavender tied with raspberry-colored grosgrain ribbon to each guest's chair make a wonderful aromatic, decorative detail when entertaining inside or out. If you first fix the bunches with rubber bands, you can leave them on the chairs as the lavender dries, giving weeks of aroma until all the flowers have fallen.*

# BAROQUE OBELISK

Evoke the sumptuous style of the seventeenth century with a magnificent beribboned obelisk. This is incredibly easy to make and the result is fabulous. However, it does use a lot of lavender and can be quite costly, so scale it down if you prefer.

*MATERIALS*
*sharp kitchen knife*
*dry florists' foam cone, about 20 in high*
*metal urn, about 12 in diameter*
*dressmakers' pins*
*2¼ yd wire-edged ribbon, about*
*2 in wide*
*12 dried poppy seed heads*
*10 large bunches lavender*

1 Using the kitchen knife, trim the bottom of the florists' foam cone, shaping it to fit snugly into the urn.

2 Using the pins, attach the wire-edged ribbon to the foam cone, starting at the bottom and working around to the top, then working back down the cone to make a trellis effect. Scrunch the ribbon slightly as you go for a fuller effect. Position one poppy seed head at the top of the obelisk and others at pleasing intervals on the cone.

3 ❧ Cut the lavender stalks to within 1 in of the heads and start by inserting in a ring at the bottom of the cone where it meets the rim of the urn. Then, working methodically in rings and lines, gradually fill in each section within the ribbons. As you get near a poppy seed head, remove it so you can insert the lavender near the hole, then replace the seed head.

# MOPHEAD TREES

Fashion a pair of enchanting lavender trees, then position them on either side of a mantelpiece mirror or fireplace in a witty allusion to real mophead bay trees growing on either side of a front door.

## MATERIALS

FOR EACH TREE

*sharp kitchen knife*
*2 dry florists' foam balls, about
8 in diameter*
*container, about 8 in diameter*
*1 yd piece contorted willow*
*5 large bunches lavender*
*florists' or gardeners' wire*
*a little reindeer moss*

1 ⊱⊰ Using the kitchen knife, cut one of the florists' foam balls in half and place in the container. Use extra foam if necessary to fill the container. Insert two 20 in lengths of contorted willow into the foam.

2 ⊱⊰ Attach the other foam ball to the top of the willow. Choose lavender with similar-sized heads and trim to 1 in. Make a ring of lavender round the foam ball, and another in the other direction.

3 ⊱⊰ Fill in each section with lavender, working in rows to achieve an even finished result.

4 ⊱⊰ Bend short lengths of wire into hairpin shapes and use to pin the moss into position over the florists' foam in the pot.

# HARVEST DISPLAY

The soft blue-green shades of dried lavender stalks look impressive when massed together in a simple arrangement. Here, they have been teamed with golden wheat and dried poppy seed heads in a tin container whose gentle gray tones offset the blues, greens and golds perfectly. If you cannot find an old tin, use any galvanized metal for a similar effect.

*MATERIALS*
*kitchen knife*
*4 dry florists' foam bricks*
*tin container, about*
*9 x 9 x 12 in*
*2 bunches dried wheat*
*6 bunches dried lavender*
*2 bunches dried poppy seed heads*
*2 handfuls reindeer moss*

1 ⚜ Fit the florists' foam into the container, using the kitchen knife to trim to size. If you are using a tall container, stand two foam bricks upright in the bottom to support the two on top. The bricks on top must fit the container tightly.

2 ⚜ Insert the wheat, a few stalks at a time, into the center of the foam. Discard any broken or imperfect stems.

3 ⚜ Working in rows, insert the lavender stalks one by one around the wheat. Graduate the height of the rows of lavender so that the front ones are slightly lower than the back ones. This gives the impression of a more generous band of lavender.

4 ⧆ Cut the stalks of the poppy seed heads to about 2 in. Insert a row all around the rim of the container. Place another row behind them so that this row rests on top of the first. Tuck the reindeer moss carefully under the front row, lifting the seed heads a little if necessary.

# VERSATILE LAVENDER

Lavender's wonderfully simple, spiky archi-tectural form makes it a natural for working into effective indoor decorations, whatever your level of skill. Whether you simply bunch it or fashion it into a complex tree, the trick is to go with it, rather than try to let it imitate the look of a traditional floral bouquet. Gather it together, stalk and all, straight and soldier-like, into bunches. Alternatively, cut off the stalks and fix the lavender heads into a base for a look that is reminiscent of the fields in full bloom.

*LEFT: This exotic gnarled lavender tree is made up of a driftwood "trunk" secured in a dish of sand, then given a mantle of dried Spanish lavender. If this seems too ambitious, try the mophead trees, or make a Christmas tree version using a cone of florists' foam wedged into a terra-cotta pot.*

*RIGHT: Bunches of lavender tied around a basket make for an exquisite, perfumed fruit "bowl." The bunches were first secured with wire, then tied with strips of Provençal-style fabric and knotted to the basket handle with small pieces of blue-dyed raffia. Adapt the idea and make a fragrant indoor decoration by attaching lavender in bunches to the rim of a basket, then filling it with a complementary potpourri.*

# POTTED LAVENDER

It is not difficult to make simple lavender arrangements in garden pots for attractive scented displays to last all through the winter. The deep indigo blues look wonderful with bright sunshine yellows, especially when teamed with Provençal-style fabrics to evoke summer days in the south of France. This pair of pots have been color-washed and then filled with flowers arranged in a neat crop to make the most of the blooms. You could vary the arrangement and make a taller display by building up a fan shape of lavender stems.

*MATERIALS*
*kitchen knife*
*1 large dry florists' foam cone*
*terra-cotta pot, about 6 in tall*
*10 dried sunflowers*
*scissors*
*1 bunch dried lavender*
*blue-dyed raffia*
*glue gun and hot glue wax*

1 Using the knife, cut and shape the florists' foam until it fits tightly into the terra-cotta pot.

2 Cut the sunflower stalks to about 2 in and insert into the foam around the rim of the pot.

3 Cut the lavender stalks to about 2 in and insert into the florists' foam to fill the center of the arrangement.

4 Tie several strands of raffia around the pot. Secure in position at the back, using the glue gun and hot glue wax. Trim the ends of the raffia.

# FRESH LAVENDER HEART

L ittle can be more romantic than a fresh lavender heart. Make one for a special occasion, then let it dry naturally as an ever-lasting souvenir. This uses a lot of lavender, so make sure you have access to plenty before you begin, or use a smaller wire base.

*MATERIALS*
*TO MAKE A HEART MEASURING ABOUT*
*12 x 12 IN*
*120 large lavender heads*
*pruning shears or scissors*
*florists' reel wire or any fine wire*
*garden wire*
*florists' tape*
*green raffia*

1 ⊰ Cut the lavender stems to about 1 in and make up bunches of about six heads each, firmly securing them with fine florists' wire.

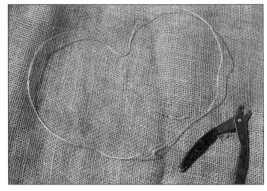

2 ⊰ Make a hook at each end of a piece of garden wire about 44 in long. Link to make a circle, then make a dip at the top edge and bend into a heart shape.

3 ⊰ Using florists' tape, bind the first bunch of lavender to the bottom of the wire heart. Place the next bunch a little further up the wire and bind that on. Continue until you reach the center top, then start again at the bottom and work up.

4 ⊰ Make a small bunch of lavender and secure with wire. Tie with green raffia. Place at the bottom of the front of the wreath and bend the stalks to the back. Pass the raffia to the back to catch the stems and then secure at the front with a bow.

# FRESH TUSSIE MUSSIE

In bygone days, ladies carried herbal tussie mussies as a form of personal perfume. They were usually made of several varieties of fresh herbs arranged in concentric circles. If you are lucky enough to find white lavender, or if you grow it in your garden, it will look great in a delightful tussie mussie when contrasted with the more conventional blue.

*MATERIALS*
*1 bunch blue lavender*
*1 bunch white lavender*
*green raffia, similar twine or rubber band*
*pruning shears*
*ribbon*

1 ✕ Arrange a circle of deep blue lavender stems around a small bunch of the white lavender. Secure with a piece of raffia, twine or a rubber band.

2 ✕ Arrange the remaining white lavender around the blue, secure the complete bunch with raffia, twine or a rubber band. Trim the stalks using pruning shears.

3 ✕ Complete the arrangement by tying on a wide ribbon, then making a generous, decorative bow.

# DRIED LAVENDER WREATHS

Lavender wreaths make for wonderful wall decorations, scenting the room at the same time. Make one pure and simple, or go one step further and decorate the finished wreath with seagrass string and feathers. The basics of wreath-making are the same, this one uses several varieties for added texture.

⤐✦⤏

*MATERIALS*
*3 bunches dried lavender*
*florists' reel wire*
*1 willow wreath base, about 8 in diameter*
*wire cutters or scissors*
*glue gun and hot glue wax*
*ribbon*

1 ⤐ Divide each of the varieties into small bunches and secure them using florists' wire. Make all the bunches before going onto the next step.

2 ⤐ Using the glue gun, attach the bunches of white lavender in two groups, one on either side of the wreath base, using the bunches to cover the full width of the base. Make a group of another variety of lavender next to each of the sections of the white lavender in the same way.

3 ☙ Continue with a section of yet another variety, and continue around, alternating the varieties until the whole wreath is covered. Make a ribbon bow to trim. Attach to the wreath with wire.

*RIGHT: The grays and browns of northern game birds' feathers beautifully complement the softened purple tones of dried lavender.*

# LAVENDER AND SUNFLOWER GARLAND

Spread a little scented sunshine with a vibrant dried garland. Use it as a celebration decoration, then drape it above shelves, kitchen cupboards or wardrobes to perfume the room for the rest of the year.

*MATERIALS*
*1 plastic garland case*
*kitchen knife*
*4 dry florists' foam bricks*
*scissors*
*10 sunflower heads*
*1 bunch dried curry plant*
*10 bunches dried lavender*

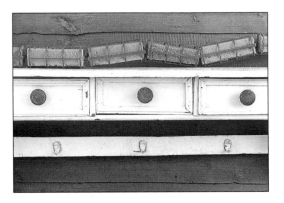

1 ⊱ The garland base consists of plastic cases that link together using a hook-and-eye system.

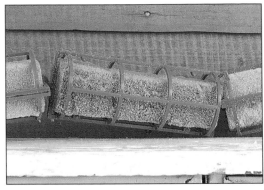

2 ⊱ Cut the florists' foam to fit inside the plastic cases, then link them together to make the desired length of garland.

3 ⊱ Position the garland on a shelf. Cut the sunflower stems to 2 in. Insert groups of sunflowers at intervals along the length of the garland. Add dried curry flowers around the sunflower heads.

4 ⊱ Trim the lavender stalks to 2 in and add them to the garland. Start by working outward from one group of sunflowers, making sure the whole area of florists' foam is covered before moving to work round the next group of sunflowers.

# SWEETHEART WALLHANGING

Create a wallhanging from a heart, roses and lavender – three icons of romance. It is very easy to make, and makes a delightful decoration for any room in the house.

*MATERIALS*
*paper, pencil and scissors*
*3 dry florists' foam bricks*
*heart-shaped copper cake pan, about*
*12 in across*
*kitchen knife*
*2 bunches dried roses*
*4 bunches dried lavender*

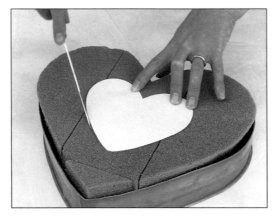

2 ⟩⟨ For the rose center, draw a heart motif onto paper and cut out. Place the heart shape on the foam and draw around with a knife to make a guideline for the roses.

1 ⟩⟨ Line up the florists' foam so it matches the size of the cake pan. Press the cake pan rim onto the foam to make a print of its shape. Using the knife, cut just inside this line so the foam shape will fit tightly into the tin. Use the off-cuts to fill in any spaces.

3 ⟩⟨ Cut the rose stems to 1 in. Place a line of them around the rose shape. Here, darker roses go around the perimeter and lighter ones in the center. Finally, add the lavender and fill in, in concentric circles, around the rose heart.

# SCENTED NAPKIN RINGS

These elegant lavender-filled organza napkin rings, inspired by a hair scrunchy, are extremely easy to make. You could make a few sets, in different colors, to suit a variety of decorative schemes or celebrations.

*MATERIALS*

*FOR SIX NAPKIN RINGS*

*½ yd metal shot organza*

*1 yd elastic*

*scissors*

*needle and sewing thread*

*loose, dried lavender*

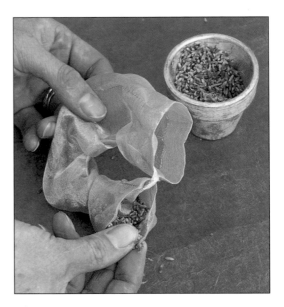

1 ⚘ For each ring, cut out a piece of organza about 12 x 5 in and a piece of elastic about 5 in or the correct length to fit snugly around the napkin. Fold the organza in half lengthwise, with the right sides together. Stitch along the length and turn right side out. Thread the elastic through the organza tube and slip-stitch the ends firmly together.

2 ⚘ Fill the tube loosely with dried lavender, then slip-stitch the open ends to each other to form a ring of lavender-filled organza.

*ABOVE: Tuck a bunch of lavender or any dried flowers or decorative leaves into the napkin ring for added effect.*

# CHAPTER FIVE

# FRAGRANT LAVENDER

———◆—▰◆▰—◆———

THE MOST FAMOUS OF THE NOSE HERBS IS THIS LAVENDER,
WHOSE FLOWER SPIKE, AS MODEST IN HUE AS A QUAKER'S
BONNET, IS HIGHLY FRAGRANT.

*THE FRAGRANT GARDEN, L.B. WILDER*

*ABOVE AND LEFT: Fresh or dried, in simple or more elaborate
arrangements, lavender brings a wonderful scent to the home
all year round.*

Of all lavender's qualities, the most unmistakable is its fragrance. The Ancient Egyptians, Greeks and Romans valued it for its perfume; the Romans used it generously in their celebrated public baths. And since then, for centuries, women have luxuriated in lavender baths, perfumes and cosmetics, besides using it dry to give fragrance to their homes all year round.

Over the ages, lavender may have enjoyed greater or lesser popularity, but it has never disappeared. Lavender is still a major player in the perfumer's repertoire. Its distinctive aroma that is both sweet and pungent, fresh and slightly medicinal, has a quality that never becomes sickly or cloying. Nowadays, lavender's perfume is associated with women, perhaps because, for most of the twentieth century, it has not been fashionable for men to use perfume. But this was certainly not always the case. The Ancient Egyptian, Greek and Roman men were just as likely to use lavender fragrances as were women. And did they but know, so are today's men!

Lavender is so useful a perfume, long-lasting as it is evocative, that perfumers use it extensively in products for men, too. Even men who do not think they use fragrances, are probably unsuspectedly splashing on the

*ABOVE: The mere sight of a lavender field in full bloom is enough to evoke its pungent perfume.*

lavender in the form of shaving creams and foams, for perfumers use lavender in much the same way as chefs use salt. Even if it is not evident in a fragrance, lavender is very likely to be there, drawing out other aromas.

Lavender water was one of the very first perfumes (as opposed to unguent) to be developed in Europe, made in the twelfth century by a Benedictine abbess, Hildegard, who wrote prolifically about plants and medicines. But perfume did not become generally used until many years later because the church did not think it seemly to use fragrances. It was not until after Henry VIII dissolved the monasteries that once again the fragrance of lavender became popular. His daughter, Elizabeth I of England, was a great devotee, paying her distillers enough to keep them secure for a lifetime for a single compound.

By Stuart times, the fragrance was being used to scent all kinds of household products, such as furniture polish, candles and even soap. It was Henrietta Maria who introduced the Continental idea of perfuming soap and cosmetics to Britain when she married Charles I. It became fashionable for the ladies of large houses to spend hours in their pantries distilling lavender oil and using it to concoct lavender waters, creams and potions. They would also dry lavender to use for "sweete bags," and as a base for potpourri to scent their rooms.

But the heyday for English lavender came during Queen Victoria's reign. She, too, was very fond of the fragrance, and used to stroll through the lavender fields in Wallington with

her appointed "Purveyor of lavender essence to the Queen," Miss Sarah Sprules, "drinking in" the heady aroma of fresh lavender in full bloom under summer skies. The essence and dried flowers allowed that perfume to permeate her different residences for the rest of the year. Floors and furniture were polished with lavender-scented beeswax, potpourri released its aroma into the rooms, lavender water and soaps perfumed the bathroom.

The queen set a fashion for lavender-scented cleaning, washing and polishing products, and soon even the most humble abode took on the fragrance of lavender. The trend took root and became a favorite of several generations. But toward the second half of the twentieth century, lavender-perfumed homes became associated with elderly aunts, and its popularity gradually waned.

Lavender is still a favorite fragrance, but lavender gifts and decorations do not have to be rooted in its Victorian heyday. There are many new ways it can be used for making gifts, or as wall or table decorations that look wonderful while releasing that inimitable aroma.

*LEFT: Lavender became a popular ingredient for all kinds of cleaning products, valued for its disinfecting qualities as well as its perfume.*

# LAVENDER PAPER FOLDS

In the sun-baked markets of Provence, dried lavender is sold in folds of brown paper. It is an idea that can be adapted easily with the help of a color photocopier, to make decorative scented sachets for cabinets, drawers or shelves. You can ask any color photocopying shop to enlarge or reduce any image to the size you want. Old labels from food packaging were used here, but almost any print would be suitable – and, of course, you still have the original intact.

MATERIALS
*tracing paper*
*soft pencil*
*scissors*
*any print for decoration*
*loose, dried lavender*
*hole punch*
*twine*

1 First prepare a tracing paper pattern measuring 8 x 11¼ in. Draw a straight line parallel to one long side, 1 in from the edge. Draw another line parallel to this about 4¼ in from the same edge. Draw a line between these two lines 3¼ in from the top, and another the same distance from the bottom. This panel shows the space and positioning for the photocopied image. Take this tracing and the print to a color photocopying shop and ask them to enlarge or reduce the image to fit the panel, printing this more or less in the middle of a sheet of paper. Position the tracing over the photocopy so the image is in the correct position. Draw around the tracing, then cut it out along these lines.

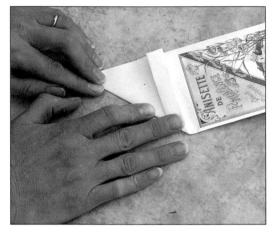

2 Make the first fold along the inside edge of the image so the paper is folded almost in half. Crease and unfold. Turn the paper over, facedown on a smooth surface, and fold down along the position of the line close to the long edge. Crease and unfold. Refold the first fold, then fold one long edge over the other so its edge meets the second fold line. Fold both thicknesses of paper in the position of the second fold. This provides a seal along the whole length of the sachet. Turn the sachet over and at one end, fold down the corner so the folded seal comes to the front.

3 Fold the top point down so it tucks into the folded seal. Fill the sachet with dried lavender from the open end.

4 Fold the open end in the same way as before. Use a hole punch to make a hole in the corner, and attach twine.

# HOUSEHOLD LAVENDER

The pantries of the past, presided over by the mistress of the house, were where polishes, soaps, perfumes and dyes were made as well as where foods were preserved and medicines formulated. Richly aromatic lavender would have had a leading role to play for many of these functions. Furniture polish may have been made from beeswax and lavender; candles would have been scented with lavender; lavender would have been hung up in bunches to dry in the pantry. Oil would have been distilled, potpourris mixed and stalks of the lavender preserved to throw on the fire to give fragrance to the living rooms. In later years, it may have been the butler who presided over furniture polishes, candles and fire sticks. Today, people are equally familiar with the scent of lavender in household products: soaps, polishes and all manner of cleaning materials, even spray air-fresheners. Much of the lavender perfume used in modern household products comes from the thriving lavender industry in Spain.

*LEFT: Save the dried stems of lavender, bundle them up and throw them on the fire for a natural aromatic room scent.*

*RIGHT: Dried lavender is a traditional ingredient for scenting furniture polish, candles, soap and a wide range of cleaning materials.*

# ORGANZA CUSHION

Dried lavender flowers, seen through translucent organza, contribute to the design of this exquisite cushion. They provide a delightful pale indigo texture while releasing their fragrance to scent the whole room. The backing is in linen, which adds weight and gives the whole cushion a wonderful feel.

### MATERIALS
*scissors*
*½ yd purple linen*
*½ yd purple metal shot organza*
*pins, needle and sewing thread*
*1½ yd wide ribbon*
*1½ yd narrow ribbon*
*1 large bag dried lavender*
*4 gold tassels (optional)*

1 ⟩ Cut out a 12 in square of linen and a matching square of organza. With wrong sides together, turn in the edges all around. Pin and baste. Stitch through all the layers, leaving a 4 in gap for filling. Measure the combined widths of the ribbons and use pins to mark this amount in from each side of the cushion. Use the pins as guides to the correct distance from the edge for stitching, leaving a gap corresponding with the gap in the first row of stitching for filling.

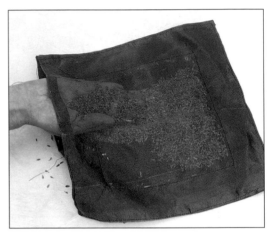

2 ⟩ Fill the middle section of the cushion with lavender. Stitch to close. Stitch along the outside edge to neaten.

3 ⟩ Cut two lengths of the wide ribbon to the length of the width of the cushion. Fold down the corner of each and crease. Trim to near the crease line.

4 ❧ Using small running stitches, hand-stitch along the diagonal close to the edge. Repeat on all four corners.

5 ❧ Hand-stitch the outside edge of ribbon to the outside edge of the cushion, then stitch the inside edge of the ribbon in place.

6 ❧ Repeat the same operation with the narrow ribbon. Hand-stitch the tassels to the corners at the back of the cushion.

# LAVENDER POMANDER

This delightful lavender version of a spice pomander makes an aromatic room decoration any time of the year or an imaginative Christmas tree decoration.

*MATERIALS*
*medium-gauge florists' stub wire or*
*garden wire, about 16 in long*
*1 dry florists' foam ball, about*
*3½ in diameter*
*wire cutters*
*18 in ribbon*
*2 bunches dried lavender*
*scissors*

1 ❧ Bend the wire in half and fix through the center of the ball. Pass the ribbon through the top loop and push down so that it is fixed firmly to the ball. Trim the ends of the wires. Bend the wires at the bottom, flat against the foam, to secure the ribbon.

2 ❧ Select similar-size lavender heads, and, starting at the bottom of the ball, push the stalks into the foam, making a circle around the circumference of the ball.

3 ❧ When the first circle is complete, make another circle of lavender around the circumference at right angles to the first. This will divide the pomander into quarters.

4 ❧ Working in lines, fill in one quarter. Repeat with the others. Tie a bow at the top of the ribbon.

# LAVENDER CANDLE RINGS

The Scandinavians have a great tradition for making candle rings from all sorts of materials to decorate the tops of candlesticks. These lavender rings make a very pretty table decoration, while adding to the ambience with their exquisite aroma. Make sure you snuff out the candles before they are low enough to burn the decorative lavender and candle rings.

*MATERIALS*
*medium-gauge garden wire*
*wire cutters*
*1 bunch dried lavender*
*scissors*
*fine-gauge florists' wire*
*narrow satin ribbon*

1 Make a ring of garden wire that will easily slip over the candle, but that is snug enough to rest on the top of the candlestick. If you do not have any garden wire, make a ring using several thicknesses of florists' wire, then use another piece to twist around the ring tightly to hold all the

thicknesses together. Make small bunches of lavender and trim the stems to about ½ in. Secure the bunches with fine florists' wire, if necessary.

2 Bind the bunches of lavender to the ring using fine florists' wire. Thread the ribbon through the wire ring at the front, then tie in a bow to finish.

# LAVENDER OIL LAMPS

Oil lamps make an original alternative to candles as a table decoration. They look wonderful grouped into an arrangement, with some standing on glass stands to create a variation in heights. By scenting store-bought blue candle paraffin with a few drops of lavender oil, it is easy to create a romantic and aromatic lamp light for the room.

1 Using the small funnel supplied with the oil lamps, pour in some blue lamp oil to a depth of about 1 in.

2 Drop in about ten drops of lavender oil, then wash through with a little more lamp oil. Be careful not to overfill the lamp.

Do not leave the lamps burning unattended and keep out of reach of children.

# RIBBON HANGING

This exquisite gossamer wallhanging is made from two shades of chiffon ribbon, woven together, then scented by tiny bouquets of lavender tucked into the pockets created by the weaving. This hanging is not difficult to make, but as the ribbon is very slippery, it is fussy and needs patience.

## MATERIALS

*6 yd chiffon ribbon in one color,
3 in wide
7 yd chiffon ribbon in another tone,
3 in wide
scissors
pins, needle and sewing thread
paper and pencil
1 bunch lavender
1 yd narrow purple rayon ribbon
1 yd narrow pink rayon ribbon
narrow copper piping*

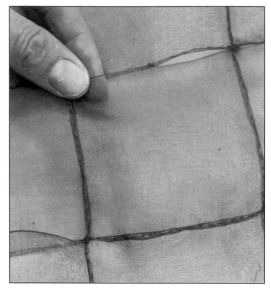

1 ⟫ In main color ribbon, cut four lengths measuring 1 yd 3 in and four lengths measuring 2 ft. In the other tone, cut three more long and four short lengths. At one end of each of the longer lengths, fold a double hem to make a casing. Slip-stitch. Lay these longer ribbons on a flat surface next to each other, alternating the colors, with the casing at the top, wrong side down. Weave one of the short lengths through the longer lengths, aligning the top edge with the casing. Make several small neat stitches at the corners where the ribbons cross. Weave through another short ribbon in the toning color and stitch. Continue with the remaining ribbons.

2 ⟫ Next, top-stitch the pockets, which not only hold the bunches of lavender, but give the hanging a quilted effect. Start by "quilting" all the verticals. Let the sides of the vertical ribbons overlap very slightly, then make tiny running stitches along the overlap. You will find you are stitching through three layers: two verticals and a horizontal. The horizontals are stitched in a similar way, except where the horizontal ribbon is at the front of the hanging, you will need to leave the tops open to make the pockets. At these points, make the running stitches just through two layers — the vertical ribbon and the horizontal one running behind it.

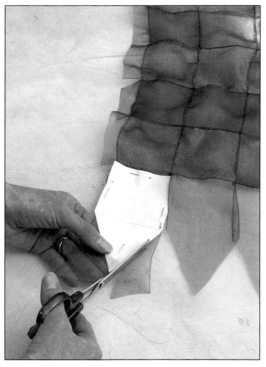

3 ᢞ Cut the ends of the vertical ribbons
into points. The most accurate way to
do this is to first make a paper template, pin
this to each ribbon in turn and cut out.
Trim the horizontal ribbons so they are of
an even length.

4 ᢞ Make bunches of three stems of small-
headed lavender and tie each one with
purple or pink rayon ribbon. Tuck them
into the pockets. Thread the copper piping
through the casing and hang on metal hooks.

# POTPOURRI IN A GAUZY BAG

Gather dried lavender heads into an exquisite pompon of metal shot organza, tied with wide velvet ribbon in a generous bow. It looks wonderful, smells wonderful and, unlike most other potpourris, it does not collect dust.

*MATERIALS*
*1 yd purple metal shot organza*
*scissors*
*needle and sewing thread*
*3¼ yd narrow rayon ribbon*
*1 yd broad velvet ribbon*
*dried lavender heads*

1 ⚜ Cut one piece of 16 in organza and four 16 x 4 in strips for the facings. With right sides together, sew a strip on opposite sides of the square. Sew the other strips to the other two sides of the square. Trim the seams, snip off the corners and turn the facings to the wrong side.

2 ⚜ Top-stitch all around the edge of the square. Use the rayon ribbon to neaten the edges of the facings: cut a length of ribbon a little longer than the side of the square, turn the ends in, then stitch in place over the raw edge of the facing. Repeat on all four sides.

3 ⚜ For each corner tassel, cut four lengths of velvet ribbon about 5 in long, fold in half and stitch another small piece of ribbon in place near the fold. Trim the ends at an angle. Stitch to the corner.

4 ⚜ Spread out the finished organza square, facing side upward. Place a handful of lavender heads in the center, then gather up all four corners to make a pouch and tie with a flamboyant bow.

# LAVENDER WATER

1 | Put 3 cups lavender and 2½ cups still mineral water into a large, heavy saucepan and bring slowly to a boil, stirring constantly.

2 | Simmer for ten minutes, remove from the heat and allow to cool to room temperature. Strain into a bottle and add ⅔ cup vodka. Shake well.

*RIGHT: Lavender sweet water has been a favorite since the twelfth century. Splash it on for a refreshing fragrance or add it to footbaths to soothe the feet at the end of a hot day.*

# LAVENDER AND BATHING

Lavender and bathing have gone hand in hand since ancient Egyptian times. Treat yourself by adding a few drops of lavender oil to the bathwater to lift spirits and ease aching muscles. When you get out of the bath, splash on refreshing lavender water.

*ABOVE: Lavender-scented bath crystals, oils and cosmetics make wonderful aromatic and healing treats after long, stressful days.*

# LAVENDER SOAP

1. Cover ten lavender flowers with ¼ cup boiling water. Infuse for 30 minutes. Strain, discarding the flowers.

2. Grate plain soap into the infusion over a low heat and stir constantly until thoroughly mixed.

3. Press the mixture into balls and allow to dry and harden. This will take at least two days. There are plenty of other lavender gifts that are easy to make, even if you do not have a lot of time to spare – the secret is in beautifully presenting bought lotions, soaps and creams.

*RIGHT: You may not have the time or inclination to make your own lavender soap, but you can still put together a charming lavender bath gift by wrapping lavender soap attractively, tying it with string and sealing with wax, then teaming it with lavender sachets in natural linen.*

# BATH BAG

H ang a lavender-filled linen pocket over the hot running tap and you will have a relaxing, naturally scented bath.

*MATERIALS*
*pencil and paper*
*scissors*
*½ yd natural linen*
*pins, needle and sewing thread*
*button, 1 in diameter*
*colored string for hanging*

1 ✻ Make a paper pattern template. Cut out one complete shape in linen. Cut a rectangle the same width as the pattern but 6½ in long for the front of the pocket. Use the pointed end of the pattern to cut a facing that measures 6 in.

2 ✻ Stitch a narrow hem at the top of the pocket's front and the bottom of the facing. With wrong sides facing, pin the front and facing to the back of the pocket and stitch all around. Trim the seams, snip the corners and the top point. Turn right side out and top-stitch all around. Make a buttonhole in the point of the flap and sew on the button. Fasten the button, then make a handle by passing a piece of string under the flap at the top and tying in a knot.

# BATH SCRUB MITT

Let the healing properties of lavender oil get to work after a hot summer's day outside when grasses, burrs and brambles have made their mark on hands and legs. Lather up the outside of this mitt with soap as normal, then tuck a lavender-filled sachet into the heart-shaped pocket. As you scrub, the lavender is crushed and releases its oils.

### MATERIALS
*tracing paper*
*pencil and paper*
*scissors*
*waffle-weave or terry washcloth*
*in navy blue*
*waffle-weave or terry washcloth*
*in lime green*
*pins, needle and sewing thread*
*fuchsia-colored stranded embroidery thread*
*½ yd colored muslin*
*dried lavender*

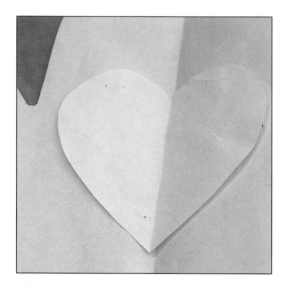

1 ⚜ Make a paper pattern by tracing the glove and heart templates. Cut out in paper. Cut any borders off the washcloths. Cut two hand shapes from the navy blue washcloth and one heart shape from the lime green washcloth.

3 ⚜ Using two strands of embroidery thread, work blanket stitch around the edge of the heart so that the solid line covers the original stitching. Stitch through all the thicknesses where the heart is joined to the mitt, and just through the heart thickness at the top where it is free. This provides strength to the heart.

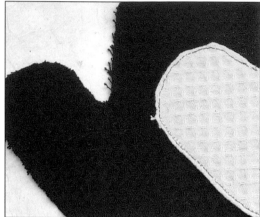

2 ⚜ Turn in the edges of the heart shape and stitch all around. Make a hem at the bottom edge of both of the hand pieces. If you are right-handed, place one hand piece right side up with the thumb facing right. If you are left-handed, place the thumb facing toward the left. Lay the heart centrally on the hand and pin at the widest points. Stitch the edge of the lower half of the heart to the mitt between the pins.

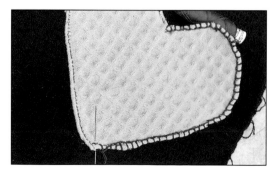

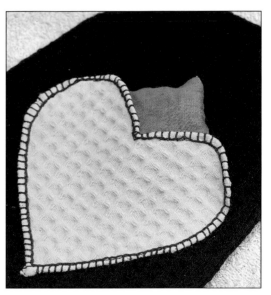

4 ⚘ With right sides facing, stitch the two mitt pieces together. Snip into the seam allowance at the curves and turn right side out. Top-stitch around the mitt. Stitch together 2 in colored muslin squares along three sides to make sachets and fill with dried lavender. Turn in the top edge of each one and stitch to close. Throw away the sachets after they have been used.

# LAVENDER TO GIVE

A gift of lavender, however simple, is always welcome. If you don't have time to make something from scratch you can buy a gift and present it in an original way.

*LEFT: These miniature painted picture frames have added appeal when each is given a tiny bunch of dried lavender.*

*BELOW: Turn dried lavender into a special gift by presenting it in a cone of cellophane tied around with a generous amount of satin ribbon.*

ABOVE: *An embroidered lavender bag and matching cushion make a delightful gift when presented in a natural wooden basket.*

RIGHT: *Pretty white cotton handkerchiefs filled with lavender and tied with gossamer ribbons make for the simplest, yet most charming of lavender bags.*

# LAVENDER OVEN GLOVE

Fill an oven glove with lavender so that you will smell its fragrance every time you pick up a warm pot or plate.

MATERIALS
*1 yd ticking*
*scissors*
*scraps of scrim, muslin or cotton*
*½ yd batting*
*pins, needles and sewing thread*
*dried lavender*

1 Cut out two pieces of ticking measuring 30 x 8 in wide. Neatly round off the ends. Then cut out six rounded pocket ends 8 in long; two in ticking, two in scrim and two in batting.

2 Cut the remaining ticking into bias strips 1¾ in wide. Make a double hem along the straight edge of the ticking pocket ends.

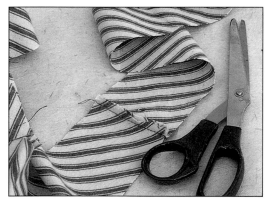

3 Stitch a batting pocket and a scrim one together. Fill with lavender. Stitch closed. Stitch the bias together to go round the glove; use a short piece for a loop. Fold a 2¾ in length of bias in half lengthwise, wrong sides together, and stitch.

4 Assemble the oven glove. Lay one ticking pocket end right side down, lay a full-length piece right side down on top of that, then the lavender-filled batting sachet and the other full-length piece right side up.

5 Pin the bias around the oven glove, right sides together. Pin the loop in position halfway down the mitt, with the loop tucked inside and the raw edges level with the raw edges of the bias and main piece. Stitch all around.

6 Trim close to the seam, and cut into the seam allowance around the curves. Turn the bias around to the other side of the oven glove. Turn in the edge and stitch again to finish off.

# CHAPTER SIX

# DELICIOUS LAVENDER

---·❈·---

THE YOUNG AND TENDER SPROUTINGS ARE KEPT IN
PICKLE AND RESERVED TO BE EATED WITH MEAT, AS
DIOSCORIDES TEACHETH.

*THE HERBALL, JOHN GERARD, 1597*

*ABOVE: Old-fashioned crystallized lavender, sweet and fragrant.*
*LEFT: In centuries past, lavender's aromatic qualities made it a*
*popular flavoring. Nowadays, it is not so commonly used, but it*
*can turn an ordinary dish into something much more exotic.*

Of all the aromatic herbs, lavender must be the most pungent, yet, in modern times, it has been largely ignored in the kitchen. It is hard to understand why – rosemary has a similar sweetly aromatic quality, yet it has earned a place in some of our most traditional dishes.

In the past, lavender has had an important role in the kitchen. Elizabeth I was particularly partial to lavender conserve, and in her time, it was not unusual for lavender to be used in savory dishes too. One reason for lavender's popularity as a flavoring in those days, it has to be said, was to disguise the taste of meat that was past its prime.

The use of lavender, along with other fancy tastes, probably went out of fashion when the Puritans imposed a simple diet, a trend that was not reversed until relatively recently when foreign travel introduced exotic flavors to the Western world.

With the new appreciation of perfumed flavors, perhaps lavender could resurface in mainstream cooking. As far as savory dishes are concerned, lavender can easily be substituted for rosemary to lend an exotic floral flavor to a simple dish. Try it with lamb or fish; in salads, savory tarts and savory breads. However, traditionally, lavender is used more

*ABOVE: Lavender can be used either fresh or dried as an aromatic culinary herb.*

often in sweet, rather than savory, dishes.

One of the easiest ways to impart its aromatic flavor to cakes, cookies, candies and desserts, is by making lavender sugar to use instead of ordinary sugar in the mixtures. If you do not enjoy baking, sprinkle lavender sugar over summer fruits or puddings for

added piquancy. As well as being used as a flavoring, lavender flowers make decorative garnishes. Either use them fresh or crystallize them, just as you may crystallize violets, to decorate summer sponge cakes or exotic after-dinner chocolates.

As the spike can be fairly woody, it is inclined to be rather crunchy and not at all palatable, so use whole flower spikes for decoration only where they can be removed before eating – on the tops of cakes or puddings, for example, or even to decorate the rims of plates and platters. Where the flowers are going to be eaten, take each floret off the stem, pinch the bottom ends out and use to sprinkle over, or even mix into, salads and desserts. The varieties with the deepest indigo shades are the most effective. Choose fully opened flowers from each spike, not only because they are the prettiest, but because these are the ones that will be most flavorful.

When using fresh flowers, make sure you do not pick any that may have been contaminated with pesticides, bearing in mind that winds can carry sprays – so check with neighbors. It is best not to wash the flowers as they spoil easily, so choose the ones that appear cleanest. There should really be no need to clean them anyway since lavender grows high

*ABOVE: Lavender sugar, used to sprinkle over fruits or in making jams and preserves, brings an old-world charm to tea time.*

off the ground, and most insects and birds avoid it. The only fleeting visitors are bees and butterflies. Pick the flowers early in the morning, when the dew has dried but the sun has not had time to dissipate the oils. If they are still damp, let them dry out away from direct sunlight as that is inclined to make the flowers open and release their precious oils. Any dampness left on the flowers will soon spoil them, making them wilt and in time become mildewed. If you are using dried lavender, make sure you buy culinary quality, which has been specially grown and packaged under hygienic conditions.

# CRYSTALLIZED LAVENDER

This perfumed decorative garnish for sweets and puddings makes a refreshing alternative to crystallized violets. It is best to take the individual lavender florets off the rather unpalatable stalks. You can do this before or after you crystallize them, depending on the variety. While well-spaced florets are easy to remove after crystallizing, you may find it easier to remove the florets of the more tightly-packed varieties, such as 'Hidcote', before crystallizing them.

Take the top stalks of fresh lavender and remove each floret. Discard the stalks, then, using tweezers if necessary, dip each floret first into lightly whisked egg white and then into superfine sugar. Leave to dry on layers of waxed paper. When they are completely dried out, you can store them between layers of waxed paper in an airtight container for up to 3 months.

# LAVENDER SUGAR

This perfumed sugar lends an exotic aromatic flavor to any sweet recipe. Make up several jars in the summer, then package them in attractive glass containers tied with ribbon to give as gifts.

*INGREDIENTS*
*1 tbsp dried culinary lavender*
*4½ cups superfine sugar*

Mix the lavender and sugar together well and store in an airtight container for at least a month. Shake well regularly. Use in cakes, puddings and summer drinks, sifting the lavender flowers out before use.

# LEAFY LAVENDER SALAD

It is not only lavender flowers that impart fragrance and flavor – the leaves do too. In common with many herbs, they have a naturally slightly hairy texture, so chop them thoroughly before use. Any lavender leaf turns a green salad into something very special – if you have access to the pretty fernlike ones, so much the better.

### INGREDIENTS
*2 cups mixed green lettuce leaves, such as lollo biondo, rocket, iceberg,*
*round lettuce and lamb's lettuce*
*1 tsp dried lavender leaves, roughly chopped*
*3 tbsp sunflower oil*
*1 tbsp white wine vinegar*
*salt and freshly ground black pepper*

Wash and prepare the salad leaves. Place the lavender leaves, oil, vinegar and seasonings in a screw-top jar and shake until well emulsified. Toss the dressing over the salad leaves and serve.

# RED MULLET WITH LAVENDER

Cook up a barbecue with a difference by adding lavender to fresh mullet for a delicious aromatic flavor. Sprinkle some lavender flowers on the coals too. Eaten alfresco, this will be a memorable meal with a delightful perfumed ambience.

### INGREDIENTS
*4 red mullet, scaled, gutted and cleaned*
*3 tbsp fresh lavender leaves or 1 tbsp dried lavender leaves,*
*roughly chopped*
*salt and freshly ground black pepper*
*roughly chopped rind of 1 lemon*
*4 spring onions, roughly chopped*

Marinate the mullet in the remaining ingredients for at least 3 hours. Drain off the marinade, removing the lemon rind. Cook on a very hot barbecue for 5 to 7 minutes on both sides. Brush on extra marinade as it cooks. The fish can also be fried or grilled.

# LAVENDER HEART COOKIES

In folklore, lavender has always been linked with love, as has food, so make some heart-shaped cookies and serve them on Valentine's Day or any other romantic anniversary.

### INGREDIENTS
½ cup unsalted butter, softened
¼ cup superfine sugar
1½ cups all-purpose flour
2 tbsp fresh lavender florets or 1 tbsp
dried culinary lavender, roughly chopped
2 tbsp superfine sugar for sprinkling

### MAKES 16–18

1 Cream the butter and sugar together until fluffy. Stir in the flour and lavender and bring the mixture together in a soft ball. Cover and chill for 15 minutes.

2 Heat the oven to 400°F. Roll out the dough on a lightly floured surface and stamp out about 18 cookies, using a 2 in heart-shaped cutter. Place on a heavy baking sheet and bake for about 10 minutes, or until golden.

3 Leave the cookies standing for 5 minutes to set up. Using a metal spatula, transfer them carefully from the baking sheet onto a wire rack to cool completely. You can store the biscuits in an airtight container for up to 1 week.

# FENNEL AND LAVENDER TARTS

Fragrant lavender combines perfectly with the aromatic flavor of fennel. These unusual and mouthwatering tartlets make an appealing summer starter.

### INGREDIENTS

*FOR THE PASTRY*
1 cup all-purpose flour
pinch of salt
¼ cup chilled butter, cut into cubes
2 tsp cold water

*FOR THE FILLING*
6 tbsp butter
1 large Spanish onion, finely sliced
1 fennel bulb, trimmed and sliced
2 tbsp fresh lavender florets or
1 tbsp dried culinary lavender,
roughly chopped
2 egg yolks
1 cup crème fraîche

*SERVES 4*

1. Sift the flour and salt together. Rub the butter into the flour until the mixture resembles breadcrumbs. Stir in the water and bring the dough together to form a ball. Roll out on a lightly floured surface to line four 3 in round, loose-bottomed flan rings. Prick the bases with a fork and chill. Heat the oven to 400°F. Melt the butter in a pan and add the onion, fennel and lavender. Reduce the heat to low. Cover with wet waxed paper and cook gently for 15 minutes, or until the onions are golden.

2. Line the pastry shells with waxed paper and bake blind for 5 minutes. Remove the paper and bake for another 4 minutes. Reduce the oven temperature to 350°F. Combine the egg yolks and crème fraîche together. Spoon the onion mixture into the pastry shells. Spoon the crème fraîche mixture on top and bake for 10–15 minutes until the mixture has set and the filling is puffed up and golden. Sprinkle a little extra lavender on top and serve warm or cold.

# LAVENDER CAKE

Bake a summer-scented cake that is reminiscent of those distant Elizabethan times when lavender was extremely popular not just for its fragrance but for its distinctive flavor, too.

### INGREDIENTS
¾ cup unsalted butter, softened
¾ cup superfine sugar
3 eggs, lightly beaten
1½ cups self-rising flour, sifted
1 tbsp fresh lavender florets or 1 tbsp dried
culinary lavender, roughly chopped
½ tsp vanilla extract
2 tbsp milk
½ cup confectioners' sugar, sifted
½ tsp water
a few fresh lavender florets
for decoration

1 ❧ Heat the oven to 350°F. Lightly grease and flour a ring pan or a deep 8 in round, loose-bottomed cake pan. Cream the butter and sugar together thoroughly until light and fluffy. Add the eggs one at a time, beating thoroughly between each addition, until the mixture becomes thick and glossy. Fold in the flour, lavender florets, vanilla extract and milk.

2 ❧ Spoon the mixture into the pan and bake for 1 hour. Let sit 5 minutes, then turn out onto a wire rack to cool. Mix the confectioners' sugar with the water until smooth. Pour over the cake and decorate with fresh lavender florets.

# LAVENDER SCONES

Lend an unusual but delicious lavender perfume to your scones – its fragrance marries well with the sweetness of summer soft fruit and makes for an elegant, romantic tea-time treat. Nowadays, the flavor can seem quite surprising, because the scented quality of the lavender permeates the well-known afternoon or breakfast pastry.

*INGREDIENTS*
*2 cups flour*
*1 tbsp baking powder*
*4 tbsp butter*
*¼ cup sugar*
*2 tsp fresh lavender florets or 1 tsp dried culinary lavender, roughly chopped*
*about ⅔ cup milk*

1 ❧ Heat the oven to 425°F. Sift together the flour and baking powder. Rub the butter into the dry ingredients until the mixture resembles breadcrumbs. Stir in the sugar and lavender florets, reserving a pinch of lavender to sprinkle on the top of the scones before baking them. Add enough milk to make a soft, sticky dough. Bind the mixture together and then turn the dough out onto a well-floured work surface.

2 ❧ Shape the dough into a circle, gently patting the top to give a 1 in depth. Using a floured cutter, stamp out 12 scones. Place on a baking sheet. Brush the tops with a little milk and sprinkle with the reserved lavender. Bake for 10–12 minutes until golden. Serve warm, with plum jam and clotted cream.

# TEMPLATES

*LEFT: Sweetheart Wallhanging.*

*RIGHT: Shaker Sachet; enlarge to 7 in high.*

*BELOW: Bath Bag; enlarge to 5½ x 8 in, with an extra 4½ in for the point.*

## TEMPLATES

To enlarge the templates, use either a grid system or a photocopier. For the grid system, trace the template and draw a grid of evenly spaced squares over the tracing. To scale up, draw a larger grid onto another piece of paper. Copy the outline onto the second grid by taking each square individually and drawing the relevant part of the outline in the larger square. Draw over the lines to make sure they are continuous.

*ABOVE: Ribbon Hanging pointed ribbon ends; should measure 3 in square, with extra for the pointed end.*

*LEFT AND RIGHT: Bath Scrub Mitt; enlarge the mitt to 6½ in x 10 in.*

# USEFUL ADDRESSES

## USA

Dody Lyness Co
7336 Berry Hill Dr
Palos Verdes Peninsula, CA 90274
(310 377 7040)
Suppliers of potpourri, fragrance oils, dried blossoms, herbs, spices, dried and pressed flowers.

Herb Shoppe
215 W. Main St
Greenwood, IN 46142
(317 889 4395)
Suppliers of bulk herbs, potpourri supplies, essential oils, herbs and others.

Gailann's Floral Catalog
821 W. Atlantic St
Branson, MO 65616
Offers a full line of floral supplies and dried flowers.

San Francisco Herb Co
250 14th St
San Francisco, CA 94103
Offers a full line of herbs including lavender.

Tom Thumb Workshops
PO Box 357
Mappsville, VA 32407
(804 824 3507)
Suppliers of dried flowers, containers, ribbons, floral items, spices, herbs and essential oils.

## UNITED KINGDOM

Cameron-Shaw, 279 New King's Road,
London SW6 4RD. Tel: 0171 371 8175
Dried arrangements with flair.

Damask, Broxholme House, New King's Road,
London SW6 4AA. Tel: 0171 731 3553
Linens, cushions, lavender bags, bath treats.

Norfolk Lavender, Caley Mill, Heacham, King's
Lynn, Norfolk PE31 7JE. Tel: 01485 570384
Lavender plants, dried lavender, distiller of pure lavender oil and seller of lavender products.

V.V. Roulcaux, 10 Symons Street, London
SW3. Tel: 0171 730 3125
A wonderful range of ribbons.

Something Special, 263-265 London Road,
Mitcham, Surrey CR4 3NH. Tel: 0181 687
0128 Wholesalers of florist's supplies who will mail order in small quantities too.

Wallace Antiques, High Street, Cuckfield, West
Sussex RH17 5SX. Tel: 01444 415006
Wonderful antique furniture and accessories for home and garden.

## AUSTRALIA

The Australian Lavender Growers' Assoc
RMB E1215, Ballarat, Vic 3352
Ph: (053) 689 453 Fax: (053) 689 175

Carol White
Lavandula Lavender Farm
Main Rd, Shepherds Flat, Hepburn Springs,
Vic 3461 Ph: (054) 764 393
Plants, Display Gardens, Lavender products

Yuulong Lavender Estate
Yendon Rd, Mt Egerton, Vic 3352
Ph: (053) 689 453 Fax: (053) 689 175
Lavender grower, plant sales (fresh and dried), lavender products (craft, culinary and cosmetic). National Registered Collection of Lavenders (more than 80 different lavenders).

Tanja Lavender
811 Bermagui Rd, Tanja, NSW 2250
Ph: (064) 940 159
Lavender grower, distiller of lavender oil, lavender products.

Monaro Country Lavender
P.O. Box 236, Bombala, NSW 2632
Ph: (064) 587 203
Co-operative of lavender growers.

Di's Delightful Plants
P.O. Box 567, Lilydale, Vic 3140
Ph: (03) 9735 3831
Lavender plants by mail order.

Bridestowe Estate Pty Ltd
RSD 1597, Nabowla, Tas 7254
Ph: (003) 528 182
Lavender farm, large distiller of lavender oil, retail outlet stocking oils, dried flowers and gift lines.

Orton Australia
RMB 4004A, Talgarno, Vic 3691
Ph: (060) 201 136 Fax: (060) 201 186
Suppliers of fresh and dried bunches of lavender, seed for potpourri, essential oil (10ml bottles).

# INDEX

## ACKNOWLEDGMENTS

No book is the work of just one person: it is always the result of the energy and enthusiasm of a whole team. My very special thanks go to Debbie Patterson for her inspiration and the sheer artistry of her glorious photographs; to Joanne Rippin for her wit and humour, for having the vision to steer this herb into fresh fields and the flexibility to let the ideas mature; to Liz Trigg for her delicious recipes; to Ann and Henry Head of Norfolk Lavender for their support and astounding energy, for supplying the most superb lavender to work with, and for checking the technicalities; to Tony Hill of Wallace Antiques for his fabulous location; to Damask for lending me wonderful lavender bags and accessories; to Cameron-Shaw for lending the evocative lavender tree on page 68 plus several containers; to Gloria Nichol, who kindly contributed the lavender candle rings from her Candle Book, and particularly to Nigel Partridge for the outstanding and elegant design of this book.